THE BLOOD

By: Susan D. Smith

By Susan D. Smith

ISBN-13: 978-1490518244

ISBN-10:   149051824X

Copyright 2013 Susan D. Smith

Cover Design by Susan D. Smith

Printed in the United States of America.

All rights reserved. No part of this book may be used or reproduced in any manner whatsoever without written permission except in the case of brief quotations embodied in critical articles and reviews. For information address the author, Susan D. Smith, 1169 Beckwith Rd., Fayetteville, WV 25840 or at mrsssusandsmith@gmail.com.

Justtaggingalongwithjesus.wordpress.com

This book may be purchased online at:
http://amazon.com
and other fine book sellers.

Bookstores and churches, etc., may purchase this book at wholesale for resale or distribution.

Thank you to my God, the Lord Jesus Christ, for the inspiration He gives me and the opportunities He's allowed me to have. Without God I am nothing so again, I thank you Lord!

&

Thank you to Bro. & Sis. Tommy Craft for listening to me, encouraging me, and pushing me to complete these books. I love y'all so much and appreciate you!

&

Thank you to my mother who always told stories to me and my friends. She encouraged us to believe, to dream, and to bring our dreams to life!

&

Thank you to the love of my life, my husband. He's always there, always encouraging me to go, to try, and supporting me. Thanks, Babe, I love you!

Other Books by Susan D. Smith

Surprised by God with Pancreatic Cancer

My Child, I've Got This

Coming Soon

Living the Miracle
(July 2013)

Two Destiny's One Outcome (Fall 2013)

Adventures of the Yellow Convertible Bug
(Winter 2014)

Cherry Blossoms
(Spring 2014)

Living the Dream
(Summer 2014)

Characters

Lesley – parents killed as a child

Matt – young preacher helping Lesley

Darlene – Matt's Mom

Darlene's Husband – Hiding in the trees

Michael – Deputy, on the run

Michael's Mother (Ella) – saw the murder on the run with him

Sherriff – Michael's father

Angels

Demons

Swat Team

Table of Contents

Returning Home 9

Home, for better or worse 25

Arrested 43

More than a ride home, a friend 57

Company and Going into the House 73

On the Run 85

Unexpected Guests 97

A place of Repentance and the Truth 113

The Plan and The Angels 123

The Apology, Angels,
and Special Forces Details 135

Preparation for Battle and finding God 145

Trusting God 157

The Battle with Angelic Hosts 169

Epilogue 177

Returning Home

Boarding the plane she was so preoccupied she didn't even notice the plane was small with only two seats on each side of the aisle. Normally she would have been in first class but on this plane it just simply didn't exist. She was able to take her seat early because she was a preferred customer. Really, she just wanted this flight to be over.

Waiting for everyone else to board her nightmare came back to her. She knew on this trip she was supposed to reach into the deep recesses of her mind and remember what had happened that night, but right now she was trying to forget that day when she was nine years old and her life changed so dramatically.

Stifling a response to the memory lurking in the deep recesses of her mind she remembered the smell of death. NO, not again, she thought to herself. I've come too far to waste time remembering the one night in my life that could never be forgotten… that fateful night.

Checking herself she then leaned her head back, sighing and said to herself, "You are going on this trip to find out what happened so you must remember all the details of that night even though it is your worst nightmare coming to life."

Closing her eyes while the plane continued to board she leaned her head against the window. Within a few moments she was lost in her thoughts. She was once again nine years old and could taste the fear she had felt when she woke up on the couch wondering why Mom or Dad hadn't carried her upstairs to her room.

Unbidden the images of that night came back to her. She could see herself walking from the family room with the big comfy leather couches and soft cream carpet, baby blue walls and the beautiful cherry wood trim. Walking through the dining room archway she saw the long table where friends and family gathered every Sunday for dinner with the table already prepared for dinner tomorrow.

Finally she could see herself standing at the bottom of the steps in the foyer. It was like she was looking down on herself as she stared up at the beautiful white staircase where she was remembering watching a stream of dark red blood slowly wind its way to her. Hauntingly, she could still hear the sounds of it coming towards her.

She could hear each drip of the blood as it wound its way down each step. The sound of the drip, drip, drip was almost too much for her to remember and then she couldn't quit looking at the vivid dark red stream. The dark red on the white stairs was sinister to look at. She felt that it wanted to take her also.

Looking down at her feet she could see her new Cinderella slippers turning crimson red. Reaching down she remembered touching the dark red stream wondering what it was and smelling it. She could still smell it. It was the smell of iron and death. She had tried everything to not remember that smell but it remained with her. Trying to stop herself, but knowing she could not, she began to climb the steps to her parent's bedroom where she found both of them. Once she was in the bedroom she saw her beautiful mother and handsome father lying in a pool of blood.

Her mother was lying on the floor face up. Her gorgeous blue eyes opened but unseeing with a hand outstretched as if she had tried to save herself but blood surrounded her beautiful long red hair. In her mind she could see herself reach down and touch her mother's face and trying to wake her up. She then heard herself scream, "Mommy, Mommy, wake up!" Sitting down beside her she held her hand and cried for her to wake up.

Recalling their beautiful bedroom with a huge king sized rice cherry bed with stairs to get into it and the fluffy white covers. Only this night the fluffy white covers were covered in red drops like someone had flung a can of paint all over the room. Mommy loved white so everything other than the furniture was pure crystal white but tonight it looked evil with all the drops of red everywhere.

Going around the room she noticed that the poker was missing from the fireplace and that it was in her Dad's hand. Then she stepped over to her daddy who was lying on the floor face down in a pool of blood. Daddy was so handsome. She could still see his laughing blue eyes and dark brown hair. He was so tall and so much fun, so full of life. He was too full of life to have been killed so senselessly.

She remembered patting his face and trying to roll him over. As she finally rolled his head over it was only to see his eyes rolling lifeless in his head. Then the blood, so much blood, everywhere, it was all over herself. How would she get it off? Then she could hear screams that just didn't quit. She must have screamed and ran.

She could not quit running, down the steps and out into the night. She had to be safe. But where could she be safe? The playhouse, but no, she couldn't go there. Something stopped her. Could she figure out what stopped her or who? Why did she freeze in her steps right outside the back door of the house?

She didn't remember but she knew it was like a hand reached down and touched her and guided her into the woods behind their house in rural West Virginia. Her life was forever changed that night. Her happy go lucky childhood ended.

She remembered hiding in the woods all night and hearing people calling out to her and dogs barking but she hadn't felt like she could come out. She finally fell asleep beside a tree that had been cut down. When she woke up she remembered looking into her grandfather's eyes and seeing the grief. She knew without asking that what she had seen was true.

In shock she had not spoken for days and finally in therapy one day she started talking. She had blamed herself. The police had tried to get her to tell them what she had seen but all she would say was that Mommy and Daddy had to go to heaven early and they will meet me there.

The police had not understood why they could not get her to tell them why she had hid in the woods all night and not come out when they were calling her. She still didn't understand it but this trip would hopefully bring all of that out.

Now she must focus on what she had to do on this trip. She had to face all of her memories and find out what really happened. Hopefully, based on her psychiatrist's recommendation facing her memories would put an end to the nightmares that she had.

She was tired of waking up crying and screaming for help. She wanted to be able to move on with her life and not be so focused on the past. It had to, because she could not continue to live like this. She needed to sleep and quit losing weight.

Her doctor had told her she was on the fast track to a short life if she continued with the pace she was on of working long hours and catnapping since she couldn't allow herself to fall into a deep sleep because of the nightmares.

After getting in his seat Matt looked at the beautiful woman sitting beside him and wondered what dragons were chasing her in her sleep as her head tossed back and forth. Laying his hand on his Bible he began to silently pray that God would touch her and give her a peaceful rest.

Looking at her outward beauty he couldn't help but wonder what would cause someone who looked like she had it all to be so restless and without peace. Noting that he had picked up on his mother's habit when she was traveling to wonder about the people seated beside them or folks that they saw in the airport. It had now also become his habit. He shook his head and thought to himself I've got to quit this I'm becoming just like my mother.

As he watched the ground pass swiftly by he remembered all the years his parents had forced him to church and how he had fought it. Now he was on his way to a small town in West Virginia to try out for the pastorate of a small church. It was a church that now only had services once a week when they could get someone to come in and minister for them.

Who knew what he might face? So much had happened in this small town that he knew to pastor this group of people would try all of the experience and knowledge he had gained with training.

He knew this woman could not be on the way to the same small town but he could hope and pray. He felt such a burden for her and her problems. It felt like she had a huge rock around her neck and couldn't get it off.

Closing his eyes he went into his inner prayer room in his mind and began to pray silently for the lady next to him. Not even knowing her name he felt a real burden for her so he really began to focus on her and praying for her. As she shifted her weight and laid her head on his shoulder he glanced down at her and marveled anew at how beautiful she was.

She had glossy red hair and a perfect pale complexion with long gorgeous legs. She had to be close to six feet tall. He wondered what color her eyes were. Would they be a beautiful sea blue or a mysterious brown?

Realizing he could get into trouble looking at her and wondering if this woman could be the one he would be blessed to share his life with. He remembered as a minister, his wife must be a prayer warrior, focused on the church and ministering to others and just based on what she had with her this woman did not fit the bill at all.

As he looked at her he marveled at her peach skin, beautiful hair and the professional way she was put together. Then he took note of the laptop case and briefcase under the seat and he knew in his heart this woman was focused on her career. Why then did he feel such a connection and burden for her?

Why would someone from a major city be traveling to Morgantown, West Virginia? It is the closest airport to many small towns. This town really is in the back of the beyond, he thought to himself.

That's what was wrong with him and why this woman was affecting him so much is that he was still in shock. Shaking his head to clear it, he wondered how he had gotten talked into even going to try out at this church. Even now he remembered his mother's plea to go to her hometown and check out the church in the small town his grandparents lived in.

This town needed a church on fire for God, she had told him, as he had argued with her saying he really felt a burden for the foreign mission field not some small town in West Virginia. She had explained to him that if any preacher could survive in West Virginia, in the mountains, they could survive on any mission field.

As she had pleaded with him he had seen something in her eyes that made him reconsider. It was a longing, to give something back for a family that God had blessed so abundantly it was time to bless someone else.

For as long as he could remember his mother had been involved with church, the things of God, giving back to the community. She told him it was like the verse in the Bible, Luke 12:48 "...For unto whomsoever much is given, of him shall be much required: ..."

That's why he was doing this. God had blessed him and his family and now it was his turn to give back no matter how miserable he might be in the beginning. Oh, no, he knew he couldn't think that way, he must be positive.

Opening his Bible he began to read as he let the beautiful redhead nap on his shoulder.

Stirring Lesley woke up and when she realized she had been napping on a stranger's shoulder, she moved quickly but not before she noticed a worn Bible on his lap. Oh, no, she thought, just my luck to be seated beside Joe religious. The last thing I need right now are platitudes in any form.

Turning she looked out the window, embarrassed that she had used this guy's shoulder for a pillow. Getting her focus she slowly turned to see the most beautiful ocean blue eyes grinning at her. Oh, no, he realized he had the upper hand she thought to herself. Putting her hand out to him, she said, "Hi, my name is Lesley Johnson. I need to thank you for letting me so kindly use your shoulder."

With a sincere smile on his face he took her hand in his and lifted it to his lips and kissed it. As he kissed her hand and looked into those gorgeous green eyes he knew he was in trouble because not only was she beautiful she smelled beautiful and had a need for love.

Seeing her shocked expression he quickly said, "My name is Matt Andrews. My mother always taught me to greet ladies with respect," chuckling, he said, "especially beautiful ones."

She couldn't resist smiling, as she said, "Now that is a new line; blaming your Mother," and laughed with him.

After talking for a few minutes he finally got the nerve to ask the question that was most pressing to him at that moment in time, "Why are you going to Morgantown, West Virginia?"

Looking at him, she thought, wonder why is he interested in what I plan to do in Morgantown and with a thoughtful look on her face, she answered, "I used to live not far from there but haven't been back since I was ten. Just time I went back for a visit. I'm sorry but I'm really tired I hope you don't mind but I need to get some work done while we're on this flight."

Bending down she grabbed her briefcase and pulled out a folder of copies of old newspapers. Trying not to look interested but still wanting to see what she was doing he pretended to be looking out the window

Sighing, she looked at him, as she pulled out a pair of glasses and said, "You know, if you're that interested in what I'm doing just ask me."

He looked at her and said, "Okay, fair enough, I'm game. What is so important to you in that folder?"

Looking back at him, she said, "Actually, it's none of your business!" Seeing the shocked expression on his face at her violent outburst she quickly said, "But I do need to share this with someone and as long as you don't start spouting religious nonsense at me I'll tell you. Is it a deal?"

Realizing the only way he would find anything out was to agree, he sheepishly nodded his head yes.

Pulling out the papers she said, "The reason I haven't been back to the small sleepy town my life started in, is that my parents were killed. These newspaper articles are of all the reports of what happened that night. My grandparent's decided I needed a change of scenery after a very rough year of trying to stay in the same house with me waking up screaming from nightmares of the night I found them in their blood."

Shaking his head he opened his mouth to speak, but she put her hand up and said, "No, let me finish this. I paid good money to a therapist to tell me I had to talk this out and you asked, so just listen until I finish, okay."

Seeing him nod his head she continued. "To this day I still can remember that night vividly as if I was repeating it over and over and then wondering what in my subconscious is not allowing me to forget. But, yet, not allowing me to remember everything. They never did find the murderer or murderers and the police always thought I was the missing piece of the puzzle. I have never been able to remember anything before I stood at the bottom of the stairs leading to their bedroom until today."

Pausing to take a breath, she continued, "I remember standing there. In my mind I can still see the stream of blood coming down the stairs and hear the drip, drip, drip as it goes down each step until it reaches where I am standing and then the smell of the blood. I can see the vivid redness of it and to this day I can still feel when I reached down to touch it. In my mind I hoped someone had broken a bottle of ketchup, but no such luck. As I touched it, it felt warm so I decided to investigate and in my robe and slippers walked upstairs trying to avoid getting the blood on me. As I followed the trail of blood it led to my parent's bedroom. I can see myself standing before their bedroom door wondering what they had done, wondering if it was another surprise for me. My parent's loved me and focused on me, so naturally I thought they had done something for me. Opening their bedroom door all I can remember is the blood, it was everywhere, and seeing them lying so still on the floor. Let me explain, the reason I said I didn't want you to say anything religious is my Dad was a minister and he gave his life to God and he died. I have to come to terms with it and I have to know why so I can move forward. In my heart I know I need peace but that is not what this trip is all about. It is about me being able to sleep all night without having the same nightmare over and over again," taking a deep breath she looked at him wondering what he would say to all she had told him.

Frantically searching his mind for the right words to speak to her without sounding like 'Joe Religious' as she had so callously suggested. He then took a deep breath and asked God for the wisdom to know how to help her without sounding churchy.

He then said, "Lesley, I can see this is a difficult time for you. I want to be there for you but I need to know exactly what it is you need. You don't want me to be 'Joe Religious' yet you can't ignore the fact that I am a deeply religious man and that is a part of me as much as your briefcase and laptop are parts of you. I need you to give me freedom to speak to you the way I would to anyone going through a situation like the one you are going through."

Looking at him she smiled slightly and nodded her head and began to speak, "I do understand what you are saying and I will try to be tolerant of your career choice and the fact it will inherently affect every word you speak. I also need you to make allowances for my situation and understand that being raised a minister's child I have some dragons I need to slay in my past before I can have a future without the haunting nightmares."

As he looked at her he realized not only was she a beautiful person on the outside she also had grit, something that was like a rare jewel to find. He finally spoke, saying, "Lesley, I am so thankful you have decided to let me help you. I hope, to be, not just a minister but a friend, to become a close friend. Regardless, of my position as a minister, I want you to treat me just as a friend, you can tell me anything in any way and I will not only do my best to help you but also to pray for you that God will protect you and open the doors of your memory so that you can finally lay all the ghosts of that night to rest."

"You're a minister. You certainly don't act like any preachers I have ever met and you kissed my hand. You know for a minister you certainly have a way with words. Now I have a question for you. Why are you going to Morgantown?"

Leaning his head back, he sighed and slowly said, "You're not going to like my answer but I am coming to look into pastoring a small church out in the country approximately an hour from Morgantown."

Finishing he looked at her wondering how she would take his answer. But she actually was interested and then said, "What is the name of the church?"

"It's the Pentecostal Church."

He stopped as he noticed her face turn gray and knew in his heart that this would be almost impossible to have a relationship with her when it dawned on him that she was the daughter of the last fulltime minister of the church he was going to go try out to be the new pastor.

Putting his hand on hers, he said, "Let me explain why I'm going to this particular place. It's an area where my mother grew up and she has always raised us to give back to the community since God has blessed us so abundantly. Actually, if I had my way, I'd rather spend the next few years in a major city before heading off to a foreign mission field which is where my real calling is but Mom insisted I at least come up and visit this church. She has drilled it into our heads, 'to whom much is given, much is required.' I'm sorry, you said you didn't want anybody being churchy on you and here I go. It's just a part of me and always has been."

Pausing, he took a breath, and then began again, "To understand me you have to understand how strong and real my mother's faith was and how it influenced me even as a small child. Why I remember when the folks at church would get wrapped up in worshipping the Lord. I loved to see their faces and watch them show how much they loved God through their worship. As a small child my mom would watch me play dancing in church like the adults and shouting but she hardly ever stopped me and only if I was about to get munched by someone in the Spirit because I was inadvertently stepping in their path. Why, I remember one night when we lived in North Carolina Mom was standing by me one second in the balcony and the next I heard this woman screaming downstairs in the sanctuary and then I saw my Mom in front of the choir loft dancing, cutting a rug and screaming. That night changed our lives dramatically. Within a year we had moved to West Virginia and she had quit her executive position with a major bank and my Dad had started going to church. That was a miracle."

Looking at him, Lesley said, "I can see this is a very important part of you and who you are. No you are not sounding churchy. It's just that I'm so touchy because of what happened with my folks and not knowing what I will find when I get there. No-one has been in the house since my grandparent's and I left almost exactly one year after that fateful night and I have plans to clean it and restore it before I sell it. I must have closure in this in order to move forward and it's one of the most difficult things I've ever had to do," as a tear slowly trickled down her face, she continued, "I'm sorry I just need some time to really focus on what I have to do in the next several weeks."

As she turned her head and looked out the window he could see the grief in her face. It was the eyes of a beautiful woman who needed to remember her past in order to enjoy her present and plan a future. As he laid his head back on the seat he closed his eyes and wondered what she would find. Then he went to that quiet place in his mind where he could commune with his God and lay the burden at the feet of Jesus that she had just shared with him.

What could he do to help her and how? Having heard the story he knew this had to have happened when she was a child and it would be almost impossible to figure out what had happened unless she was able to unlock the memories that her mind had blocked from that eventful night. He just hoped and prayed, it wouldn't be too much for her to endure. He also wondered what other people would think of her returning to that area to solve the murder.

The murderer could be a very influential person in the community by now and if he remembered the story right that his grandparent's had told them was that it was rumored it had to do with drugs and the fact that a revival had broken out in that small town and was changing lives, lives that sold drugs. This had made the folks over the drug trafficking mad and they had struck out at them. He knew that they may have shattered her family but God had changed people in that community and had brought a great revival after her parent's deaths.

Home, for better or worse

Feeling the wheels of the plane bump the pavement, Lesley brushed her hand over her face and realized she needed to dry off the wetness from tears that had fallen without her knowledge.

When will this end? She thought to herself. When do I get to move on with my life? Reaching for her purse she felt a hand press a handkerchief into hers and looked into Matt's concerned blue eyes.

Feeling the jolt of awareness of him touching her she quickly looked away taking the handkerchief she murmured a quick thank you. Composing herself she handed him back the handkerchief and said, "You really know how to treat a woman."

Thinking of the length of time he had spent in prayer over her he thoughtfully said, "No ma'am, you are very much a lady. One I would like to get to know better. Let's not let our meeting end with this plane trip."

As he watched her eyes fleck with questions he quickly said, "If you're uncomfortable telling me where you will be perhaps I'll just give you my information that way you can contact me should you need someone or just need to talk. I want you to know I would very much like to take you to dinner."

Realizing what had slipped out Matt wondered where that had come from. Until she had a relationship with God he had no right entertaining thoughts of her romantically, now what would he do?

He had just asked her out and knew that as a minister he could not be seen dating someone who didn't even like church or wanted to be associated with church or allow someone to talk religiously to her and he had asked her out. How was he going to get out of this one? In his mind he was saying, "God help me!"

Watching his face she saw the astonishment on it when he realized he had asked her out. Looking at him she quickly said, "Matt, you're probably not going to believe this but that Pentecostal church you're trying out for was the church my father was the pastor for a few years. Yes, I was raised Pentecostal. Am I a Pentecostal right now? Not really, but I have never quit going to church just never found a reason to really serve God after my parents died and believe me I tried. It's like I have to figure out the mysteries of my past before I can move on in any aspect. Also, perhaps, I'm afraid to truly love so I build barriers because I'm afraid that everyone I leave will desert me. I know they won't but you have to understand where I'm coming from. Yes, I'm extremely successful except for where it really matters which is why I've taken a hiatus from work. Yes, I will work from up there but only part-time for the next few months. That was one of the hardest decisions I have ever made but I must do it. I see all the questions in your eyes and I will answer them, just hold your peace. Yes, if you're willing to smudge yourself by dating me, the one considered the wild child, than I am definitely interested. Would I be an asset to your ministry? Not in this lifetime. Would I hinder you? Yes. Would you help me? Definitely," pausing she glanced up into the face of the stewardess who was waiting on them to exit the plane and turned to Matt and said, "I think they want us to get off the plane."

As they disembarked off the plane and into the small airport in Morgantown she headed straight for the rental car agency while he stopped because he had a welcoming committee. Looking through his welcoming committee he watched her at the rental car counter and wished he could be with her but since he couldn't he sent up a silent prayer for her.

Turning to the folks who had come out to greet him he quickly introduced himself and found himself staring into the same eyes he had just looked at on the plane, a hand was placed in his and an elderly gentleman said, "Son, she's my niece that you just got off the plane with and yes she has my eyes. It's a family thing. But you need to stay far away from her. You see, boy, bad things happen when she's around. I can't imagine why she would come back. I had planned on letting you rent her folk's old place, oh, well, now I'll just have to go to

27

plan B. I hope you know what an outhouse is, because that will be something you will become familiar with in the next few weeks."

Clapping him on the shoulder the elderly gentleman continued, "By the way, son, my name is Lewis Singletary and this here's my wife Leota. We are both so excited to have you coming. We ain't had a preacher in a very long time. I really hope you'll stay."

As Matt watched the elderly gentleman he had a feeling that for some reason Lesley's uncle was a force to be reckoned with and had played a major role in her past. Tuning back in he caught the last of what Lewis was saying to him, "Well, ya, hungry, that's why we came to meet ya. Do ya need to get ya a rental car or are you going to rely on us to get you around. We're not going to be able to take care of your every whim ya know."

Smiling Matt replied, "Sir, I would never depend on anyone. I have a car reserved so if you'll just give me a few minutes to take care of that I will gladly spend the evening with all of you." As he walked over to the rental counter he saw Lesley get her keys and walking up to her, he said, "Here's my card with my cell phone number. Please feel free to use it at any time. I will be there for you and I will be praying for you."

Looking up at him, she smiled back at him, noting the way his dimples creased his face and the laugh lines at his eyes, she thoughtfully said, "I'll say this for you, with that crew over there watching your every move, you are one brave man for talking to me. They all know me and think I'm almost as bad as the devil. I wish you good luck in trying out for this church. In all my years I have never felt a need to pray but I definitely will pray for

28

you. Thank you for listening on the plane and for reaching out to me."

Without thinking she just felt a need to reach up and touch his cheek, it was like time stopped as she felt the connection she felt on the plane with him intensifying. Before he could respond to what she had done she grasped his card in her hand, turned and walked out to where the rental cars were.

Knowing the area she had rented a 4x4 Electric Blue Hummer so that she could get around. Not knowing what she would face when she reached her old home she decided to stop at the nearest Wal-Mart and purchase cleaning supplies, fabric, sewing machine, patterns, some groceries and then onto Home Depot.

Even though she was exhausted and in her heels and suit it was time for Home Depot, paint, sanders, hammers, nails, nail gun, and miscellaneous parts and pieces. As she loaded everything up into the Hummer she wondered how his dinner was going and how the rest of his evening would be.

Realizing that she hadn't eaten anything all day she knew she must take care of herself so that she didn't get sick. Shaking her head she realized what she was doing even if she was doing so unconsciously. She was putting off the inevitable so she decided to go through a drive through for some food.

Once the shopping was done going back just couldn't be put off any longer. Getting into the Hummer she laid her head on the steering wheel and tried to gather strength from within herself for the journey she had ahead of her.

Unbidden a memory of her mother praying for her when she awoke one morning as a little child, knowing that prayer would give her more strength she cried out, "But I can't pray, I refuse to pray until I figure this out and can forgive God for taking my parents especially when they were working for You, God. They gave you everything and you took them from me. I don't care if it rains on the just and the unjust alike, I was an innocent child God and I deserved better", she screamed aloud.

Seeing people looking at her strangely she wiped her hand over her face and smiled. Sitting up she put the key in the ignition and automatically started it without even thinking about it. Driving to her childhood home wrapped up in her thoughts she ignored everything. As she was winding around the roads she did not notice the beautiful mountains, streams, or wildlife she was driving past. It was all lost on her.

As she put on her blinker to turn down a side dirt road a deer leaped in front of her. Hitting the break she came out of her daze and stared at the beautiful buck as it continued on its way.

Continuing she had another turn off down a path almost since no-one had come to the house once she and her grandparents moved away. As she got closer to the house she began to shake and cry uncontrollably. For some reason every time she thought about what happened or came close to the home where it all happened her body betrayed her no matter how many counseling sessions she had been to.

Driving down the road she saw the house through the trees. So beautiful, a white two story Craftsman bungalow with a porch that wrapped all the way around it with black trim and black shutters. Even without any maintenance done on it in years you could still see the white paint through the trees. She put the brake on and putting the SUV in park, she could hardly breathe, suddenly everything went black. Hearing pounding on her window, she came to and looked into Matt's face.

How had he known she would need him? She didn't know why but she was grateful he was there.

Rolling down the window, she said, "You sure are available. I didn't even have to dial your cell number."

Looking at her, he could see how difficult this was for her, and said, "I thought you shouldn't be alone coming in for the first time so I did dinner knowing you needed supplies I knew I had time. Everyone in these parts knew about this house and what happened so finding you was not a problem."

As she stared at him she thought this man could become the dearest man on earth to me and that is the last thing I need right now, "Matt, if you will help me get into the house and set up for the night I would really appreciate it," pausing and taking a long breath, she then said, "but then I need to be left alone to face this on my own, I must do this by myself."

Nodding he said, "I do understand, I just thought it might be too difficult for you tonight."

Sitting up, she said, "Let me get out and walk the rest of the way. I need for you to drive my SUV up to the house." As he got in the SUV he looked at her and said, "Are you sure you'll be alright?" As she nodded to him he drove up to the house.

31

Looking at it he wondered at the stories it could tell of the events leading up to that horrible night and what had precipitated it. Looking in the rear view mirror he watched for Lesley, seeing her walking slowly looking everywhere but at the house almost like she was avoiding it.

Suddenly she looked up and stopped. She fell to her knees and screamed a blood curdling scream. That scream sent shivers down his back and made the hair on his neck stand up. He doubted he would ever forget the sound of her screams. Closing his eyes he began to pray because he wanted to respect her wishes to do this by herself. After about fifteen minutes of listening to her scream and cry he realized she couldn't quit screaming and now she was sobbing uncontrollably again.

Getting out of her Hummer he raced to her, his heart pounding, he got to her and got on his knees and pulled her close. Based on his study of medicine before he went into the ministry he was afraid she was going into shock. That would not help her but delay her healing process.

Holding her, he prayed as he had never prayed before with desperation for God to help her. All he could say was, "Lord, please help us in Jesus Name. I plead the blood of Jesus over this home and this family!"

Staying on their knees he had no idea how long he held her but when she came to and quit sobbing she shook her head back and forth. Shaking her he said, "Lesley, snap out of it. You are okay, it is not that night. Come back to me. Talk to me!"

Finally she responded and said, "Oh, no what have I done! I should have never come back here. They tried to tell me this was a mistake. Look at me I can't even make it to the house!"

Trying to stand up they both realized their legs were numb from the knees down. They sat down, and stretched out their legs and leaned back on their hands. Matt, realizing she needed to get her mind off the past and onto the present said to her, "You know this is a beautiful place. Even though it has been neglected it's secluded with a pond in the back...."

Before he could continue she sniffled and said, "Oh, yes, I remember when my Dad put the pond in. He went to Florida and bought all kinds of different species of fish to put in the pond. They should still be there, well, not them, you know but the same species just a different generation. My uncle has been fishing in the pond and taking care of it for my grandparents. Let's walk back there."

Standing, finally that they had their legs back, they walked slowly around the property to the back of the house avoiding the house and trying to keep her distracted from the house where all the memories of that night were.

Looking at the big tree and the little playhouse someone had built for a little girl long ago, paint faded but he could still see it had once been lavender with pink shutters and a pink door.

Someone had put a lot of time into that. It even had a loft and glass windows. There was even power to it. How awesome! As she became aware of the little playhouse she ran over to it and her eyes sparkled with delight.

"Oh, Matt, I am so glad you are here, so glad I have someone to share my good memories with. My Dad and I built this together. He let me help cut wood, nail, sand, oh, he just let me do everything!" she gushed excitedly, "Dad loved me, I was the son he never had. Oh, how am I ever going to go in the big house… oh, I have to get a grip! I have to grow up! I'm not nine years old, anymore!"

As she paused Matt quickly said, "No, you're not nine years old anymore but you have never come back here since you were a child to face those memories and now you are. In your mind you are still the little girl who left here under a shadow of disaster. This has to be the hardest thing you have ever done. The only way to do this is to let it flow, take your time. As long as you get in the house tonight it will be okay or perhaps you could stay in your playhouse tonight and go to the big house during the day so you have time to face the memories of that fateful day. Stay in your little house for the night and relax, remember the good memories and I will come back in the morning with breakfast."

Letting her know he would be there for her he pushed open the door to her playhouse, even though it had been built for a nine year old child evidently her father was very thorough and made sure it was tall enough for someone at least 6 feet tall to go in and as he looked up in the loft he noticed it had not been disturbed in years.

Turning back to her, he said, "Do you have clean linens with you?"

Watching her nod her head, he said, "I'll go get them and make up the loft bed for you and make sure the power is on and that the lock works."

It was very hard not to go to her and hug her. He wished he could hold her but he knew now was not the time, now was when he needed to focus on taking care of the everyday tasks. As she watched him walk away to gather the linens it took everything in her not to run after him and beg him not to leave her alone but she knew she must face this alone.

Bending down to walk into her playhouse she remembered the small kitchen in the back of the room that had been built. She remembered her father had even purchased a used dorm refrigerator and put it in for her. Thankfully, she knew she could survive without ever entering the big house but tomorrow she must.

Sinking down on the built in sofa, breathing in the musty smell of a small place being closed up for years, she closed her eyes and in her mind could see her parents and herself in here fixing up each room and the excitement with which it was done. It was the best part of her birthday.

Out here in the playhouse, with no phone, her parents were completely hers. She did not have to share them with anyone. She knew they loved her but sometimes she resented the times they had gotten called away for emergencies and she had to be left with sitters or folks in the church. She knew she was important to her parents but it seemed the church always came before her.

Matt walked in and realized Lesley was so lost in thought she did not hear him come in. Climbing up into the loft he made the bed and as he came down the ladder she saw him and smiled up at him. "Matt, I'm so sorry, I didn't hear you come in, forgive me. I could have made my own bed. I'm just so wrapped up in so many emotions and I really don't know how to get a handle on all of it."

As he looked at her he said, "You don't have to get a grip right now. Let's clean this place up. We can start by opening all the windows. I already opened the ones in the loft. I saw a bunch of cleaning supplies in the SUV. I'll go get them and we'll get cracking. By the way I also brought my leftovers. I had a feeling you might not stop to eat."

As they cleaned they talked and got to know each other. She occasionally would go down memory lane. Once they finished and were grimy she looked at him and said, "Now what do I do? Oh, wait I know there's an outside bathroom for when Dad would come in all wet and muddy from the woods so he wouldn't track in the house. I'll use that."

They headed out to explore outside the found the outdoor bathroom right beside a workshop. As she saw it she reached into her pocket and found the key ring and opened it up. Walking in she realized everything was just as it was before his death. Dust covered every project he had been working on. She looked at him and said, "It's like stepping back in time. I can't believe they didn't do anything with all of this?"

As she touched some of the projects he had been working on, the tears started falling down her cheeks unbidden. Looking at him, she said, "I would have loved to have some of these things through the years. Why didn't they let me? What was wrong with them? Didn't they know I needed a link to my parents?"

"Lesley, it was a tough time for you. You have to remember it was tough for them also. They had you but they didn't have you. You weren't the happy go lucky child you had been. You had problems. They didn't know what they were doing or how to help you."

Picking up a book stand that had carved angels in it she said, "Let's Go."

As they walked back to the playhouse and went inside he was standing before her, gazing into those gorgeous green eyes. He knew he could go swimming in but he knew he had to focus.

So he grabbed her hands in his and said, "Lesley, I know you don't want churchy but before I leave you this evening I need to pray for you. Not because of you but for me. I hate to leave you alone. I know you must face this by yourself and I have no idea of the many emotions and thoughts that must be plaguing you but I want you to know I want God to surround you with His love and His protection."

Nodding her head she could not answer him because no-one had ever told her that in such a way with such emotion, watching him close his eyes she kept hers open for a moment and then closed hers to listen as he began to pray.

He said, "Lord Jesus, it's Matt here with Lesley. Lord, we love and thank you for all you have done for us today, allowing our paths to cross and us to share parts of our lives with each other. Father, in Romans 8:28 it says, 'And we know that all things work together for good to them that love God, to them who are the called according to His purpose.' I trust you in this matter. Now, my new friend Lesley has many things she has to work through and needs you to also be her best friend like you are my best friend. Her parents sacrificed their lives for you. So tonight we're asking, please surround her with your love and protection and allow her to face the memories of her past with her hand in yours, Father. Now let her sleep like a babe in its mother's arms tonight but let her be resting in your arms I pray. I thank you for taking care of us again, Amen."

Opening his eyes he looked at her and noticed the tears streaking her cheeks and falling onto her neck. Cupping her chin in his hands he lifted up her face to meet his eyes and he said, "It will be okay, trust in God."

She looked at him and said, "I want to, I really, really want to I just don't know if I can."

He nodded his head and said, "I understand, I hate to but I must go now. Be sure to lock the door after me."

As he left he marveled at the wonder of what he had felt at this place. Standing outside the big house he wondered at the many secrets it held and how she would deal with those secrets as they were revealed to her? Would it be too much? Would she never be able to deal with the truth?

How would she handle it? What if the truth was as horrible as she thought it was? How can I help her, God? What can I do for her? What can I do to help her find your way back to you?

Shaking his head he knew he would have to be in continual prayer for her and this situation. In the meantime he would also need to do as much research as he could about this and see if anything that had hit the media would be of any help to her.

As she stood in the door and watched him walk away from her she wondered how he had known she would need him. She remembered in her child's heart that God had sent her someone this evening. Feeling the deep darkness of the place she walked back inside and quickly locked the door. She didn't know why but she felt like someone was watching her, someone that wanted to hurt her if she remembered that night.

Sinking down into the sofa she took a deep breath and then looked down and noticed a Bible on the floor. Picking it up, she opened it and saw the name on the inside, Matt. Why did he do that she wondered to herself?

In the back of her mind she knew why he had done that. He knew that it would be hard to sleep and he wanted to leave her a book that would provide the peace and protection she so desperately needed since he could not stay with her.

Smiling she saw a note sticking out of it and opened the Bible to that page and read, "Lesley, I know I haven't known you long but all the answers you need are in this book. You don't have to be churchy just love God and love Him with all of your heart. I will be praying for you tonight that you sleep like a baby and I'll be there for you tomorrow to help open the house."

Looking down she realized he had placed his note at the favorite chapter in Psalms, "Yea, though I walk in the valley of the shadow of death I will fear no evil for thou art with me, thy rod and thy staff they comfort me...." She then noticed in the margin he had written, turn to Romans 8:31.

As she flipped the Bible to the specific verse he had left for her she read, "What shall we say then, if God be for us, who can be against us?" Feeling calmer than she had all day she looked in the margin and realized he had not written anything else. Leaning her head back on the couch she closed her eyes and let the memories of her parents and better times come back to her until she lightly dozed.

Hearing a noise she jumped up. Looking around she wondered what had woken her. Turning on the lights and looking out the windows into the black night she couldn't see anything. So she quickly changed and turned the lights out and climbed up into the loft.

Curling up with the blanket she began to pray not only for herself but for the little girl within her that was trembling in fear. Would she ever feel normal? Did she even know how to feel normal? What was normal?

As she prayed she felt a warmth come over her and a peace like she had not felt since before that fateful night. Closing her eyes she fell into a deep dreamless sleep for the first time in a long time.

Arrested

Rolling over Lesley went to raise her head and nearly bumped it on something. Opening her eyes she looked around and tried to remember where she was and then it all came back to her and she groaned.

Then she remembered how good she had slept, almost like she had lain in someone's arms. Turning over she looked at her playhouse and remembered the good times, the fun she and her parents had when they had built it and purchased the furnishings and linens.

So much to remember of the good, she hated to think about remembering the bad but soon she had to do it, in order to lay it to rest and get on with her life.

Stretching she just wanted to enjoy the quietness of the morning. Taking a deep breath she knew she had to get up and start this day.

Climbing down the ladder from her loft bed she remembered the food she had brought with her and seeing the doughnuts on the table she went for the little fridge and got the milk out.

Taking the doughnuts and milk she went into the little living area and sat down on the overstuffed window seat with faded blue gingham fabric her mother had recovered, the beautiful white walls with little blue roses her mother had etched and looked out on her old home. This should be a safe and tranquil place. Tucking her fluffy robe under her feet, she leaned back on the cushions in the window seat and relaxed.

Looking at the big house she wondered why it seemed to be looking menacingly towards her and could not figure it out. Pulling her robe closer she knew she must get dressed but suddenly felt like she was being watched. No-one should be here and no-one should certainly be lurking around the house but me.

Jumping up and quickly grabbing clothes she rushed into the bathroom and pulled on a long jean skirt and an old college jersey. Pulling on her tennis shoes she wondered what she would find when she stepped outside
.
Hearing someone knock on the door of her playhouse she called out, "Who's there?"

Not hearing an answer she looked out the peephole her parents had insisted be in the door to see a policeman.

With the chain on the door she slowly opened it and said, "May I help you, officer?"

"Open the door, Ma'am, You are trespassing and I need to take you to headquarters," the officer replied.

"No sir, I am not trespassing. This is my home. My aunt and uncle have been taking care of it for me. I came in last night on the plane and drove in from Morgantown. I would love to open the door but need you to hand me your badge. You see where I live we trust no-one, uniform or no uniform, so I need to see your badge and then I need to call your Chief and confirm you are indeed an officer."

"Ma'am you have no rights as you are the one trespassing. If this truly was your home you would have stayed in the house and not in a child's playhouse."

Replying to him she said, "Sir, if this is my home and it is, then I have news for you, no law says I must sleep in my home. I can sleep anywhere on the land I own. Now, hand me your badge please."

As he slipped the badge through the opening in the door she studied it and said, "Okay, I'll open the door, hold on."

Opening the door she took the chain off and opened it and said, "Now what is your problem?"

Looking at her down his long lanky nose he said slowly as if she was a slow child who did not fully understand, "No, Ma'am I don't have a problem but you do. This place has been vacant for years. The family has the law patrol here every day to assure no-one is vandalizing the place. Now I come and find you living in the

45

playhouse and a huge SUV parked outside that only a millionaire could afford to drive. I don't know about you but I see a problem with that. Now do you care to explain yourself?"

Looking back at him as if he was dense and not an officer of the law she said, "I am the owner of this property, or rather, if you are smart enough to understand I am the child of the parents who were murdered in that house and now I am back to solve the crime that the local police were unable to almost twenty years ago."

Her voice began rising to a near scream from all the stress she had been under with all the nightmares, she said, "Maybe you can explain why a one horse town with policemen who are more interested in people moving into abandoned homes than a double murder investigation that has not been solved for over twenty years! Care to explain that one officer!"

As he looked at her he said, "That's not the issue now, I need proof that you are who you say you are. Do you have the deed or a copy of it with you? That would prove that you have permission to be here."

"Now, think officer!" She screamed feeling exasperated with him, "Do you really think, in your evidently slow mind, that any sane person would carry a deed worth over two hundred thousand dollars around with them. Oh, wait, that's right you can't think that high. Small towns with people who think they are big fishes are the worst kind. God help us if these people actually had any real power in a town of any size they might be dangerous. Of course I don't have a deed or a copy with me. Do you take me for a fool?"

"No, but evidently you take me for one," he said, eyeing her clothing, "Now, turn around slowly and put your hands behind you….."

She interrupted him saying, "You really think you're going to arrest me like a common criminal! Fine, go ahead and do it," she screamed shrilly, "But I'll have your job for this!"

"Now, Ma'am as it is right now I've only got you for trespassing but keep this up and I'll add resisting arrest to the charges, that is since I'm not so smart I might have to think up something like assault on an officer with a deadly weapon."

Whirling around before he could fasten the cuffs she raised her hand into a fist and hit him as hard as she could. Making contact with his face, she realized what she had done she began shaking with anger as she looked at his shocked face and said through clenched teeth, "Just put the handcuff's on me and let's get this over and done! Make sure you lock up my play house. My father built it for me for my eighth birthday present!"

Standing her up and turning her around he noticed her red face and eyes that spit anger at him. Realizing he had not read her, her rights she continued to berate him and talk, "… about how in Mayberry, USA people did not know how to exist or could survive in the real world… had never been outside Hicksville, USA and did not even know how to speak proper English!"

Finally he had, had enough! He was about to lose his temper. He realized this was going to be a long day and he was going to have a shiner he would have to explain.

He did not want to tell anyone a woman had swung at him and blacked his eye.

Oh, no, what was he to do, so he just walked her out to his cruiser noticing the brand new Hummer in the driveway. He opened the back door of the cruiser and told her to bend her head and he helped her into the car and still she continued ranting at him, finally he interrupted her saying, "You are now considered a suspect in an investigation and I wish you would be quiet."

Smiling up at him but with anger gleaming in her eyes she said, "You may dream of peace and quiet but I will haunt you at night and you will hear my voice screaming at you to solve a crime of over twenty years ago and quit harassing an innocent victim of that crime who has come back to do something the police could not do <u>over twenty years ago.</u> Did you hear me? I said, they could not do their job over twenty years ago, now what makes you think you can do your job today? I mean, you could not even keep me from hitting you"

As she paused for a quick breath, he sighed, and thought about how today was supposed to be a slow day, no excitement just a few routine rounds and then lunch at the café and then paperwork and finally home. Oh, Lord, he thought to himself, what I would give for that lady in the back of my cruiser to shut up.

As he drove into town he ignored her ranting until he heard her say, "Did you hear me, I said, I want an answer from you as to how a police department could be so unreliable and unprofessional as to let a crime, probably the only crime that had been committed in years stay on the books for twenty years? Now what is your answer to that question!"

As he turned into the police station he calmly said, "Ma'am it's your crimes I'm interested in at this moment, not anyone else's."

As he opened her door she thought to herself, oh, no this is not the way I wanted re-introduced to my hometown. Keeping up her act of being the hurt victim and using her most shrill voice she continued berating him as he walked her into the station.

He said loudly to speak over her, "You'll be booked first and then appear before a magistrate."

Knowing even if she had squatted at her home she would get off with nothing since he had forgotten to read her, her rights she said to him, "I do get a phone call."

Nodding at her he said, "Yes, as soon as you are booked."

As he walked her through the booking procedure he took off her handcuff's and she said as she rubbed her wrists and saw the bruises on them, "I need to file a complaint for police brutality and harassment."

He looked at her and laughed, a laugh from his belly and said, "Ma'am in no way have you been brutalized or harassed if anything you have harassed me."

"As I just said, I want to file a complaint but first I need to call my lawyer."

He snickered and said, "A lawyer on a Saturday, now I know you are crazy."

49

Smiling sweetly she said with saccharine in her voice, "Oh, but I have his cell number and trust me he'll answer."

Nodding he said, "Okay, I hope you can call him collect because we don't allow long distance calls on our phones unless you have a calling card, but, then you didn't bring your purse with you."

Laughing up at him, she said, "Oh, but I know my calling card number by heart." She paused as if explaining to a very small child, "You see, when you have to travel internationally you learn to memorize the important numbers just in case of an emergency. So, please lead me to the phone, now!"

As he led her to the phone she wondered just what her attorney would think of this fine mess. He had told her before she left the city that this was a mistake and she should just let bygones be bygones. He had also told her that her parents were religious fanatics and whatever had happened to them should prove to her that God was not real and would not be there for her. But there was something in her, something that knew the God her parent's had served was real. Somehow figuring out this whole mess would prove to everyone that God is real!

Reaching the phone she picked up the receiver and began to dial her calling card number when she suddenly realized the pay phone in the police station was not push button but the old rotary dial. She would have to go through the operator, hearing him chuckle behind her she thought to herself, just wait, I'll turn the tables on this local bozo and fix him.

Once she got through the operator and heard Ned's voice pick up on his cell she said, "Oh, Ned, I'm so sorry to bother you on a Saturday but I'm in a spot of trouble and need your help."

Before she could say another word he said, "Tell me you didn't go to that hick town, please, tell me you didn't. I really thought you were smarter than that. Oh, no, what did you do?"

Taking a deep breath, she calmly said, "I've been arrested for trespassing on my parents property and the deputy is unwilling to believe me when I told him who I was. Anyway, I need you to fax me a copy of the deed to my parents place with all the receipts for back taxes that have been paid through their estate."

"Alright, I can do that but I need to know exactly where you are and the arresting officer's name and rank. I'll get them faxed to you today."

"Let's see his name is, oh, he never gave me his name. Oh, yes there is one other charge you need to know about, resisting arrest…."

As Ned sputtered she said, "Before you ask, yes I did resist arrest because he was acting like King of the Manor or something and I wasn't taking it off some twerp in a small town who I could buy and sell many times over."

Sighing loudly and rubbing his balding head, he said, "Just how much trouble are you really in?"

"Ned, I swear, that's it. I didn't think when I went to hit him that it would actually land. I think I gave him a black eye."

Shaking his head, he wished he had not inherited this client from his father but said, "Okay, is the officer listening to all of this? Did he read you your rights?"

Thinking for a moment she said, "Yes he's listening, he's actually standing right behind me. Come to think of it, I don't think he read me my rights."

Smiling Lesley said, "We got him, right, he has to let me go."

Shaking his head again, he said, "Lesley, the police don't have to do anything but exactly where are you?"

"I'm at the jail in the county seat. The officer is here now if you need to speak with him."

Thinking that he might be able to repair some of the damage she had done to the local police he said, "Yes."

Introducing himself as the legal counsel for the estate and for Lesley Nichole Johnson and explaining that he did have a copy of the deed and as Lesley was the only child of the deceased he would fax it to the police station later in the day. Then he needed to know the magistrate's name or what could be done about the other charges.

The deputy said, "Sir, we can dismiss the other charges with proof that the house is indeed her family home, however, you might want to instruct your client in the proper way to handle oneself when finding oneself on the wrong side of the law."

Chuckling Ned said, "Yes, sir. If you could please let me speak to my client again, I would appreciate it."

Grinning to himself, he thought Lesley would go ballistic if she knew he thought this was funny….

"Ned, Ned….are you there?"

"Yes, Les, I'm here and it looks like my kindness is getting you out of another fine mess you've made. I'm to fax the deed and the trespassing charge will be dropped. As for the other, if I were you I'd apologize to the officer, because he said he would also drop the resisting arrest charge."

"Really, Ned, do you know he put handcuffs on me and paraded me through town like some common criminal. I have bruises. We need to see about slapping this office with a police brutality lawsuit."

Interrupting her he said, "Aw, we don't want to do that and you really need to apologize to him now. With these charges dropped you will be fine with no worry's and if you ever decide to marry me than we can secure our political future. I cannot afford to have a wife who has a police record."

Shaking with anger she screamed, "Ned is that all you think about. Politics!"

Gaining control of herself, she then said, "Please fax the deed and I'll think about whether or not I will embarrass you."

Feeling someone pecking her shoulder she said, "Yes?"

"You have to get off now you've gone over your time limit."

Signing she said, "Gotta go, Ned. Hicksville, USA has a time limit on calls. Remember the number for faxing. Thanks."

Hanging up, she said, "Okay, I'm sorry, now what?"

Looking at her he said, "Let's start over, my name is Officer Michael Davids and you are?"

Now you want to know who I am, she thought to herself, but calmly said, "My name is Lesley Johnson. I am in the area indefinitely to solve my parent's murder."

As he calmly discussed with her the murder he asked why she thought it was a murder and she explained what she had found on that night when she was nine years old. She also explained about the nightmares and how she could not remember the details.

As he mulled over everything she had told him he decided he should look into it but also advised her saying, "You should leave this alone. You could be putting yourself in danger by digging up things. Let us do it for you. This way it will be safer and you can go back home knowing I am taking a personal interest in your case."

Shaking her head, she quietly but very firmly said, "No, this is not negotiable. I have to know what happened that night and be able to sleep again. I have not slept totally sound since that night over 20 years ago until last night and I refuse to let anyone or anything keep me away from the truth."

Hearing the fax machine pick up he knew he had to let her go once he saw that deed and without it he had no case. What was his father, the Sheriff, going to say when he heard about Lesley? He knew information in her parent's case had been buried and his own father had done it. Oh, which way to go now?

Seeing the deed he picked it up and realized if he wanted to he could keep her in jail for the weekend until he could confirm the deed but that would probably only give her more reason to find out the truth. This is going to not only open up a can of worms for the police but for some of the wealthiest of the community including the Mayor.

Walking over to her after reading the deed and confirming the receipts were copies of originals from his courthouse he said, "You are free to go. Is there someone you would like to call to come and pick you up?"

Shaking her head, yes, he then led her to a phone and she called her one and only friend in the area, the preacher, Matt. What was he going to say when he found out why she was calling him today?

More than a ride home, a friend

Hearing his phone ring, Matt pulled it out of his pocket and said, "Hello." Lesley quickly said, "Hi, Matt it's me Lesley. Remember we had a date for lunch."

Shaking his head he couldn't remember anything about having lunch plans with Lesley but before he could say anything she quickly said, "You won't believe where I am or what I have spent my morning doing."

As she explained what had happened and that she desperately needed a ride home he quickly said, "I'm on my way. It'll take me about half an hour. Sit tight, okay?"

Smiling she hung up the phone and went to sit down on the bench in the hallway while she waited on him.

Officer Michael Davids walked up to her and said, "You know, I could have taken you home and you wouldn't have had to bother anyone."

Looking at him she said, "No, I want to be with him and he is very willing to pick me up. If it's not against the law I'll sit here and wait for him."

Nodding his head yes the officer said, "Good luck on solving your parent's murder."

As he turned to walk away from her he realized he needed to spend some time with his father understanding the unsolved case of Lesley's parents and why it was so important to have swept it under the rug all those years ago.

Walking outside he got into his cruiser and drove quickly to his parent's house in the country. Once there he knew it would take some doing but he had to have all the pieces of the puzzle before he could figure out how to proceed. He knew getting those details out of his father would be like pulling teeth.

As Lesley sat waiting on Matt she wondered what was going on. She was getting all kinds of strange vibes from the officer that arrested her. He seemed too intent on her staying out of any reopened investigation. But he just didn't understand she didn't have a choice she had to take care of this in order to move on.

Hearing someone clear their throat she looked up. She found herself looking into the face of an elderly bald stooped man with horn rimmed glasses and many wrinkle. The scars on his face made his squinty eyes look evil, chilling her to the bone.

Then he started speaking in a menacing voice saying, "Hello, dearie. You're new to the area. I couldn't help but overhear part of your conversation with the officer. You do know he is right about the police handling everything. When individuals, like yourself and family members decide to start their own investigation they usually end up getting hurt. Wouldn't want anything to happen to that pretty face, now would we?"

Shocked she looked at him and as he began to speak again she wanted to run but couldn't, As he patted her on the face with his old gnarled hand he said, "You do know when you open a can of worms they do sometimes lead to unexpected people that you might even know and love. Wouldn't want to have one of them getting hurt in the process now, would ya?"

Interrupting him she said, "Are you threatening me? I don't take kindly to threats."

Answering her, he said, "Nah, sweetie, this ain't a threat it's a promise. Bad things will happen to the little woman who won't keep her nose out of things that don't concern her just like your parents!" He then stalked off out the double doors.

Watching him walk away she knew he held a key to all that had happened all those years ago but would she live to find the answers? She had known people would oppose her snooping around but nothing had prepared her for less than twenty-four hours after arriving home that someone would walk right up to her and let her know how dangerous this might be for her and the ones she loved.

Shaking with fear and anger she saw Matt materialize through the same doors the man had just walked out. When Matt saw her, he could see her face was bright red and her eyes were flashing dynamite, he said, "Lesley, what is it? What's wrong?"

As she explained to him about the man and asked if he had seen him come out of the building he said, "Yes, I did see an elderly man walking down the steps as I was coming up. That's who threatened you. He looked harmless. We must find out who he is. No-one has a right to threaten you. They were your parents and if you want to find out the details about their death and why the cops haven't caught the killer yet. That's your business and no-one else's!"

Looking up into Matt's face she could see he was visibly shaken by what she had told him. Neither one of them noticed the elderly man watching them from behind the tree beside the sheriff's office.

Walking towards his car they both became lost in their thoughts. Matt was wondering why it was so important that people wanted the investigation to remain closed and unsolved. Looking at Lesley beside him he knew she needed a friend and he felt that God wanted him to be that friend. Oh, but this was going to be one of the hardest assignments God had ever given him. He knew he could very easily fall hard for her, not only was she beautiful but she needed him in a way no-one had ever needed him before.

Lesley noticed Matt had stopped walking and was staring at her. Looking up at him she said, "Okay, what is it? Do I have something on my face? Are you upset that you had to rescue me from a jail cell or are you getting ready to tell me you can't be there for me?"

Smiling at her he said, "No, Lesley, nothing like that. I was just lost in my thoughts trying to decipher everything you told me that happened in the past twenty-four hours. It sounds like a bad nightmare. Ahh, shoot, I'm sorry, I know it happened to you and I know you still have nightmares about that night but we will get to the bottom of this. I promise you."

She looked up at him and said, "You don't have to stick your neck out for me like this. I'll understand if you want to just walk away. I really don't want to be the reason you don't get to be the pastor of that church and for someone you just met."

Shaking his head back and forth he said, "Nah, no way, I'm already in too deep. I know I shouldn't tell you this but I really like you and I need to do this."

As they got in his car she happened to glance over and see the Sheriff watching them, she shivered. As she wondered what was the big mystery that no-one wanted uncovered he pulled out.

Looking across the road at Lesley and the new Pentecostal preacher he wondered what connection they had to each other. Knowing he had to go to his folks and confront his father he wondered what would be said and what he would have to do. Once he reached his parent's farm which was close to Lesley's old home place, he paused in the car wondering how he was going to start this conversation.

Even though he had never been a praying man he laid his head on the steering wheel and said, "God, I know you don't know me and I got no right asking you for anything but I really need wisdom right now to know how to handle my Dad and this situation."

Brushing his hand across his eyes he raised his head and stretched as he reached for the door handle in the cruiser and slowly got out of the car. I am not looking forward to this, he thought to himself.

Starting up the car, Matt looked across the road at the police chief and saw him with his head bowed and he said a silent prayer for him. Looking next to him he saw Lesley and knew God had a reason for him to be here and Lesley was a big part of it.

Feeling that she needed contact with another human being he placed one hand on top of hers in her lap and said, "Lesley, you've got a friend in me."

Not understanding the mystery and the silence surrounding her parent's death he knew within himself he had to help her and he was glad he had called his mother to have her pray. As he smiled at her he said, "Hey, what about some lunch and forget about what happened this morning. Let's just spend some time getting to know one another."

Meanwhile, Officer Davids, was dreading the conversation he was going to have in just a few minutes with his father. As he pulled in the driveway, he saw his

Dad sitting in the porch swing reading the paper. Stepping out of the car, he took his hat off and put it in his hands, walking up the steps, he heard his father say, "Why are you home at this time of day? I thought you were on duty until midnight!"

Understanding that his father's gruffness was his way of letting him know he was worried about him, he smiled slightly, and said, "It's okay Dad. I'm here on official business."

"What do you mean, boy?"

"Dad, I need to talk to you about an unsolved murder case."

"I thought I told you, never to bring that case up."

"Dad, their daughter has a right to know who killed her parents and why."

"No, she doesn't. It will just stir too many things up. More murders could happen."

"What do you mean? More murders…."

"Exactly that, more murders," and he stood up and went into the house slamming the door.

Not wanting to but knowing he needed to, he followed his father into the house. Seeing him his mother stopped him and said, "Son, what is going on here?"

"Ma, nothing you need to concern yourself about. It's just police business."

"If it's about that preacher's daughter who came back to town and opening up that house where those murders were, I can tell you, now, that is bad news!"

Turning her back to him, she stomped away, muttering under her breath. As he watched her, he stood there shaking his head wondering what had gotten into his parents. They were the ones that always forced him to face things, yet he couldn't get them to give him a straight answer about this.

Wondering if he should pursue this with his father he decided to let it rest for now and called out to no-one in particular. "I'm going back on patrol, talk to you all later."

Driving off he began to wonder why no-one wanted the case re-opened. He thought it has to be someone close to me that was involved or someone important that everyone is covering for. As distracted as he was he hadn't noticed the car following him down the deserted stretch of road lined with apple trees until it gunned its motor and sped up beside him.

Looking over at the black sedan as it passed him he saw a sawed off shotgun coming out of the window. In shock he couldn't believe what he was seeing and almost didn't duck in time.

As the first shot went over his head he pulled his service revolver out. As he heard the next shot rip into the car door and hit the seat he raised up and shot back but not before they fired off another shot and hit him.

Feeling the searing pain he knew he was hit but that he needed to defend himself so he continued to shoot back. Finally, he saw them speed off and instead of letting them go he gunned his motor and took off after them calling for assistance at the same time. No-one came back to him and he knew he was on his own.

Why wasn't anyone answering his calls for help? There were other officers on duty. Unless someone thought he knew too much and they wanted him out of the way. This is way too creepy he thought to himself as he continued to chase the black sedan. No-one knew what was going on or what had happened this morning except for the people in the office and his dad, the Sherriff.

Could his father be involved? No, his father upheld the law. Didn't he?

Wondering how long he could continue with blood dripping down his arm he continued to race after the sedan. As he rounded a curve onto a straight stretch it was like the car had vanished into thin air. Knowing that couldn't happen he stopped his car and listened for noises and hearing none he began to search through the trees.

Still finding nothing he drove himself to the hospital. As he went in the doctor and nurses were in shock. Gunshot wounds typically only happened during deer season. As he passed out he heard them tell someone to call his parents.

A few hours later as he was coming to he saw his mother's tear stained face and grinned. "Guess what, I got my first on the job injury, Ma!"

As she looked at him with tears streaming down her face she said, "Son, I've never said this to you before but now I must. You must leave this case alone. If not, you will be killed. Today was a warning. It's up to you what you do but for my sake and your father's don't do this."

Even though he was feeling the effects of the medication he looked at her and said, "Where's Dad?"

Shaking her head she said, "Don't ask me that just please do what I ask."

Trying to stay awake, his mother took her hand and touched his face and said, "Sweetie, just sleep. I will be here when you wake up." Letting the medicine take over he drifted off.

Sitting there beside her son she began to remember the night of the murders. She had told them she would come and visit their church and had been to the house that night for dessert and Bible Study. Driving down the road she had been one of a few witnesses that could identify the car and the men on their way to the house. But before the police could question her she had been silenced and would continue to remain silent.

They had threatened her son. The one thing she loved the most and would give her life for. She knew she should tell what she knew but fear had kept her silent. She wondered how different her life would have been had she spoke up.

Her son would not be alive now but it still might cost him his life. She knew that influential people in the area had gotten upset because that Pentecostal church was costing them money because people were getting saved and not going to the bars or doing drugs anymore.

Holding onto her son's hand she was thankful that a guard was outside the door but no matter how tired she got she would not leave his side. She knew these people were ruthless and would stop at nothing to stop this investigation being reopened. Laying her head on his bed she drifted off.

Hearing a noise she raised her head and saw the door being opened by a priest. This was not her local parish priest but a strange priest.

Screaming loudly she said, "Get Out, Now! Security, help!"

Hearing no-one coming to her aid she grabbed the water pitcher and threw the water at him. Seeing him stunned she grabbed her purse she had loaded down and threw it at him. Seeing his hand with a needle in it she knew she had to protect her son.

Racing around the bed she didn't notice that her son was coming to. Seeing his mother in danger he summoned all the energy he could find and let loose with a yell and kicked the man in the stomach.

Grabbing his middle he heard an alarm outside and ran out the door. As the doctor and nurses came running into the room his mother with wild eyes looked at her son and said, "Are you ok?"

Nodding his head he let her know he was fine. As the nurses began working on him and the doctor began to question his mother.

She knew something wasn't right with the staff and she asked them where the officer was that was stationed outside the room and they said his shift had ended and

67

he had gone on home. The sheriff had decided security wasn't needed.

As the realization dawned on her that her husband had decided to protect not his son and wife, but the mafia, she knew she must get her son out of town fast if he was to make it through the night. Wandering where to turn next she finally began to pray.

Even though prayer hadn't helped that preacher and his wife that night she knew from the way they lived that they truly believed in the power of prayer so she thought maybe twenty years later it just might help.

Lying in the hospital bed Michael pretended to be sleeping but watched his mother grab his hand and begin to talk, "God, if you're up there, I need you and Michael needs you and even though his Daddy doesn't think he needs you he does. We are in a heap of trouble and someone is out to kill my son. Now God twenty years ago I didn't do what was right but it's time even if it might cost me my life just please don't let it cost my son's life also. I know I'm a selfish opinionated old witch who doesn't deserve you to give her the time of day but God I need you now! Tonight. I remember in that Bible study I went to that Pentecostal preacher saying to plead the blood of Jesus when things were desperate. Well, I think you'd call this desperate so I plead the blood of Jesus. I don't understand how this will help but it certainly can't hurt so please God help us."

Opening her eyes and seeing Michael looking at her in shock and disbelief that his own mother had not spoken up and knew something incriminating about those two unsolved murders was just about all she could take.

Knowing she had to say something to him but not knowing where to begin she paused.

"Mom, why haven't you said anything?"

"Son, it's not as simple as you think. What we must focus on right now is keeping you alive and getting you out of here because they are out to silence you one way or the other and knowing your father they have decided to kill you as a warning to him."

"What does Dad have to do with this?"

"We can't waste time thinking about things like that right now but how to keep you alive. We must write everything down because this room, if it isn't already, probably will soon be bugged and they will hear our every word."

Hearing a knock on the door and seeing the nurse come in with medicine for her son, she quickly reached up and grabbed the medicine and said, "I'll make sure he takes it."

"Ma'am I have to see him take this," the nurse responded gruffly, "I will not leave until I see him take it"

Hoping that Michael could see in her eyes that even the medicine could be dangerous she handed him the cup hoping he would do what he did when he was a child and would hide the medicine in his cheek and pretend to swallow. He was a real pro as a child doing that.

As he put the medicine in his hand he could see the fear and warning in his mother's eyes and tried to remember what she was saying, then he remembered and knew what he must do even though his arm was throbbing and he could really use some pain pills right now

As the nurse closed the door to his room and walked out he spit the pill in his hand and said, "Now what?"

Shaking her head she said, "Son, let me fluff your pillows and you rest."

All while she was in her purse getting a pen and paper and writing to him letting him know that she was getting his clothes and going to get him dressed and that they must leave. They had to, now, before anything else could happen even though she didn't have a clue where they should go or how. She knew better than to use her cell or any phone in the room. She hoped for someone anyone she knew to come and visit so they could sneak out with a friend but they had to go now they couldn't wait no matter how dangerous it would be.

Company and Going into the House

As Matt drove back to Lesley's place after lunch he realized she had focused on him and finding out what made him tick while they had lunch. That was fine but now he didn't know much more about her than what he'd learned on the plane. Oh, well, now they were loaded down with cleaning supplies and more groceries to go to her place and finally go into the house and freshen it up so she could start staying there tonight.

As they pulled down the driveway, well, pathway he noticed that it seemed like several cars had been out that way. Not wanting to frighten Lesley but needing to let her know he cleared his throat and touched her arm saying, "I think you've had company while you've been away today."

Drowsily looking around she noticed the same things he had and wondered who would venture to her parent's house. As the car came to a stop she saw several cars in the driveway and wondered what was going on.

Matt hadn't told Lesley but he had phoned his mother after he had left her last night and told her the story. She had insisted on coming to be with Lesley, telling him that with all the controversy and the initial warning he had received she would feel better if she stayed in the house with Lesley. He had tried to convince her not to come but seeing all the cars he now knew he had failed miserably at that.

Looking at Lesley he sighed and said, "There's something I should tell you. You see last night I was so worried about you I prayed the whole way to where I'm staying and felt like I should talk everything over with my Mom. Well, it's kind of like, this, my Mom is a take charge kind of person. I think all of this is probably because of her since that's her Durango parked over there."

Lesley looked at him in shock and said, "You mean to tell me you let your elderly mother come up here to help me when this could be considered dangerous. Are you out of your mind?!"

He started laughing hoping she wouldn't say that to his mother. No-one called her elderly and lived. Even though she was over sixty now she still had the energy and drive of a twenty year old and even with a career in business she had somehow managed to write several best sellers and become a motivational speaker.

Oh, and, he thought to himself, this is going to be explosive because my mom has enough attitude to put Lesley in her place. Wondering what he was thinking when he called his mom he knew this was going to be exciting.

Knowing she was distracted he quickly responded, "Well, let's go see what's happening. It looks like all of these people got into the house somehow."

As they got out of the car and quickly walked up on the porch he saw his mother coming toward the door. He knew this was going to be awkward but he had no idea until he saw that most of the people that had met him at the airport were in the house. Lesley's eye's got big when she saw all of them but, she thought, what can I do?

As Matt introduced her to his Mom he could see the shock on Lesley's face when she saw that his mother didn't look much older than him. He chuckled to himself that she had called his mother elderly. Oh, boy would his mother ever be upset if she knew that.

Then he thought he heard respect in Lesley's voice when his Mom put her arm around Lesley to hug her and said, "Honey, when I heard what had happened to you and the warning Matt was given at the airport. Why I just took vacation for a while because I feel like you need someone in your court. I called my friends who pastor in the area and found out some of the wonderful names of the folks that attend the local church and I called them and told them we needed to help you out. That's what your parents would have wanted and they would have been ashamed that these folks didn't offer that last night."

Lesley was getting dizzy just listening to Matt's Mom. She believed he had said his mom's name was Darlene. Now as she was being introduced to everyone she noticed that most folks seemed to be genuinely nice and wanted her to feel at home. They had uncovered the furniture which for the most part was worn and old but in good condition. She then walked into the dining room with Darlene and saw a smorgasbord of food fit for any board meeting and her mouth watered. Eating lunch with Matt she had spent more time staring at him and into those bedroom blue eyes. She had spent more time watching as that one piece of hair kept falling over his eye and he had to keep swiping it out of his face than she had eating. Smiling to herself she knew she needed to eat.

Unbidden an image came back to her of Christmas when her parents must have had a church party and the table had been full of food and the house full of laughter. A tear slid down her face and she knew she needed people here today.

Turning to everyone Lesley said, "Have you all eaten yet?"

As she saw them nod no she said, "Well, we've got a minister so why don't we bless the food and eat. Then we can get to work."

As they ate she found out that a couple of women worked at West Virginia University in Morgantown and another one was a lawyer. This made her feel better about being here to stay for a while. This would be the perfect place for her write her next bestseller.

As they cleaned she found one dear old lady who remembered all the parties her parent's had hosted when she was a small child. She was able to give Lesley a sense of family and heritage. This lady was called Mama affectionately by everyone it seemed. Even though Matt was not by her side most of the day she would glance at him and it would center her world.

That evening as everyone left except for Matt and his Mom she wondered where Matt was staying and if there would be room for his mother there. Knowing the house was huge and his mother had brought new sheets and comforters for the bedrooms and towels for the bathrooms she felt like she should ask her stay when she heard Darlene tell Matt, "Honey, here's my keys I need you to get my luggage out of the Durango and ask Lesley which bedroom she would like me to take. Now I know you slept in the rental car last night but you can't continue that so tell me what arrangements have been made for where you plan to stay."

Matt answered and said, "Mom, you can't expect Lesley to let you stay here she needs time alone to remember without a lot of noise and as for me I'll be fine…."

Interrupting him she said, "So, in other words that mean old man who was supposed to have arranged a place for you to stay has not done so and you will be living in that tent you told me you were buying today. I don't think so. No son of mine will sleep in a tent even if it is good training for a future missionary."

Lesley couldn't help herself from laughing when she heard Matt's gasp at what his mother had said about the tent. Coming closer, she said, "I expect both of you to stay here. There is plenty of room and with your mom here, Matt, we should be well chaperoned but if it is a problem you could always sleep in the playhouse."

Darlene seeing the sparks between her son and the gorgeous redhead said, "Mmmm, this should be interesting. Lesley, I hope you know why I planned to stay with you without asking. Yes, I am overbearing and I feel that you are in a situation you have no control over at this point and there is strength in numbers. Also, I thought with this house being so remote that we should have protection which is why I drove instead of flying. I brought some items for us to use for target practice. I felt we might as well sharpen our hunting skills in case we need them later."

"Ma, tell me you didn't bring some of Dad's guns. You know you can't shoot worth anything, you're more dangerous with a gun than without."

Hitting his head with his hand he said, "Ma, how am I going to protect you from yourself? Have you forgotten the fact that someone big doesn't want her parents murder case reopened? They could come calling with a machine gun! You could shoot yourself trying to shoot them!"

Lesley was getting tickled watching Matt and his mother. It was really hilarious. His mother's face was turning red and when she looked at him you could see flames in her eyes when she said, "Well, I don't know about that but I do know that you should be more afraid than whoever might shoot us because right now I'd like to take many years off your life and I am thinking snatching you bald would do the trick. Oh, and by the way I didn't want to say anything about this until everyone was gone but did you ever think that your father could resist a fight. Where do you think he is right now? Don't say anything but think about that, would you?"

As realization dawned on Matt he made a circle with his mouth and his eyes grew big as he now knew he might not see his Dad this trip but he was close and he was armed. This also meant his Dad had given his Mom a refresher course in guns but expected him to make sure they became expert shooters. Oh, why had he called her last night? Right now he was regretting it because he had planned to sleep in his tent in the woods in sight of Lesley's house in case she needed him but now his Dad was probably out there and had probably snuck in without being seen.

"So, Dad went to that computer show again?"

"Yes, Matt he did and I don't know when we'll hear from him. You know how he is about technological stuff. He gets all wrapped up in it and forgets the time."

Lesley was looking at both of them like they had lost their minds. One minute she could have sworn that Matt's mom was letting him know his Dad was here and the next minute they were talking about a computer show he had gone to. She looked at them questioningly and Matt just shook his head and put his finger over his mouth to mimic shhhh.

Now she was really confused, what was going on? Suddenly it hit her they thought someone might have bugged her home. She became livid and wanted to tear the house apart. Matt could tell by the look on her face the thoughts that were going through her mind and he said, "No, we don't want to rearrange the house tonight. I know Lesley, that you have ideas about placing the furniture but I'm really tired. We've had a full day and I think we all need a good night's rest."

Knowing what he was doing and knowing that Lesley hadn't yet ventured upstairs but had made sure people had taken care of cleaning everything Darlene said, "Lesley, sweetie, would you like us to walk you upstairs so we can figure out the sleeping arrangements?"

Lesley nodded her head and walked over to the beautiful staircase. This house is really a showplace she thought to herself but it has seen so much tragedy. Putting her hand on the mahogany post at the bottom of the stairs she looked up to the second landing and thought about how gifted her father must have been to have built such a beautiful home.

Gasping she looked down at her feet and could see blood dripping towards her, a steady stream surrounding her feet. It's like she had no control over the memories. As her eyes glazed over she slowly started up the staircase as if in a trance.

Matt and Darlene saw where Lesley's eyes had diverted and looked down and realized she must be remembering so they kept quiet. As Lesley slowly took one step after another she climbed the stairs and ended up in her parent's bedroom. It was just as she remembered it. Not one thing had been changed. She walked over to the closet and saw that her mother's clothes were still there.

She remembered after the funerals when she and her grandparents had moved back into the house she had been adamant that no-one could sleep in her parent's room and because she had been the one to find them they had given in and taken the bonus room for their bedroom to make it easier for her.

As Matt and Darlene watched her from a distance she suddenly came out of the master bath and sat down on the floor by the bed. Tears were running down her cheeks as she wondered if she would ever remember what it was about that night that still scared her.

He sat down beside her and put his hand in hers and Darlene had followed and sat down on the other side of Lesley and took her other hand. Looking at her son Darlene saw he wanted her to start so she said in a quiet tone, "Lesley, honey we'd like to pray with you. In the Bible it says where two or three are gathered together I will be there or something like that. At my age my memory is going."

Smiling Lesley looked at her through the shimmering tears and said, "I understand what you mean and yes I would love for you and Matt to pray for me."

"Lord Jesus, tonight we are in a strange turbulent environment but we know that all things work together for the good to them that are called according to your purpose. We also know through the Word that you neither sleep nor slumber and that you are not hard of hearing. Now God we really need you to hear us close tonight. Our sister, Lesley, needs peace tonight and a sanctuary in her childhood home. We know that you can give that to her and we know that you will protect us as we sleep and send your guardian angels to protect us. We praise you, Jesus, for dying for our sins and for all that you have done to us but most especially for answering our prayers before we can pray them and providing what we have need of. You are such a great God and glorious I could never thank you enough for all you have done for my family and what you are going to do for Lesley. Lord, I know I'm being wordy but difficult times call for difficult prayers. Lord, I ask you to forgive us of any sins we may have done today and I thank you for that forgiveness. I pray, Lord, that if I offended anyone today that you will bring it to my mind so that I can go and make it right with them. Lord Jesus, you are such an awesome amazing God and I love you for taking care of us."

Pausing his mother opened her eyes and looked at Matt and said, "Okay now Matt it's your turn or Lesley can go."

Looking at Lesley Matt said, "When I was growing up we would lay in bed and say what we affectionately called our nighty night prayers and the way we would do this is that Mom would start and then my sister and I would each take a turn. She made it fun for us but made it an important part of our day to talk to God like He was our best buddy."

Lesley looking at Matt said, "Okay, I'll go next."

"Jesus, I know you're there. I just don't have much faith. I haven't been very faithful in my prayer life and feel guilty asking for anything. God I want you to know how thankful I am that you sent me Matt and his mom. I don't think I could have done this without them and I know that was one of those prayers you answered before I prayed it. Now, I ask that you protect all of us and all of Matt and Darlene's family as they have come to help me. I only ask that you help us solve this mystery. I know that you know what happened here and what it is I must remember. Jesus, help me to remember."

Opening her eyes she looked at Matt and nodded that she was through. Matt didn't know how to begin but he said, "Lord, I love you and thank you for this evening and for your Spirit that I feel here tonight. I am awed by your presence and by how you provide for us. We need you tonight in a tangible way and you are here. As Mom used to say when we were kids, heavenly father we thank you for the guardian angels you have dispatched to protect us so that we can sleep in peace. We love you so much Jesus."

As he opened his eyes he looked at his mother and winked and she began to sing, "Hallelujah, Praise ye the Lord, Hallelujah, Praise ye the Lord," until they all started laughing.

Matt said, "Lesley, part of our prayer routine was Mom singing us into giggles so we would go to sleep happy. Now we can all rest in God's peace in our beds and I know that I have officially become 'Joe religious' and that is what I promised I would try not to be but this is just a part of me."

Smiling at him she said, "I know and it was wrong of me to ask you not to be who you were meant to be from birth and if my parent's had lived who I might be today. Now, let's get unpacked so we can get some sleep and someone check all the doors and windows and make sure they are locked."

On the Run

As darkness cloaked the outside of the hospital that night Michael watched his mother sleeping and knew somehow he had to get her to safety. If his life wasn't worth anything anymore he hated to think of his poor defenseless mother being in the same predicament. Nothing had been said about what had happened all those years ago and what his mother had seen. He wondered just how involved his own father was as the police chief for the county.

Now that he thought about it he couldn't remember his father ever losing an election or even coming close to losing. He also remembered how on the years his father had opponents running a campaign on honesty and morality somehow they always ended up moving or disappearing altogether. Thinking to himself, he wondered if his own father was part of the drug problem that had plagued the county for years.

Seeing his mother stirring he knew he had to think about how they were going to get out of the hospital without being seen. Also how were they going anywhere if the cars had tracking devices planted on them? Well, he thought, if it means our safety we might just have to steal a car to get out of here and to somewhere safe.

Looking over at him she marveled at her son and wondered how they would fare in this web of deceit and immorality. If he only knew that his father not only is part of the local mafia but the head of it he would likely kill his own Daddy. She had protected her son from his father's evil ways for years and now it was time to pay the piper but somehow without letting him know who ordered the hit on the preacher and his wife twenty years ago.

Looking at his mom he said, "Good to see you finally woke up. I'm really thirsty. Can you get me some water?"

As she filled his glass she looked at him and said, "Michael how are you feeling?"

While they continued to talk about mundane things they were writing notes to each other about what to do and where to go. Finally, Michael was shaking his head. He couldn't believe his mother was recommending they go there for safety instead of running hard and far away.

Shaking his head no she looked at him and wrote, "Son, the only safe place is where they won't expect us to go and that is back to the scene of the original crime."

They waited until after midnight and the nurses doing their rounds and they got dressed. Well, Michael's mom tied his gown tighter and found his shoes for him to wear. He looked a sight. A 240 pound man over 6 foot with a hospital gown on and standard issue shoes from the county police and his petite 5 foot 2 inch mother. As quickly and quietly as they could they headed out to the stairs and down to the first floor and out to the parking lot. Once they left hospital grounds he asked her, "Mom, why didn't you come forward all those years ago?"

"Son, I know now I must but first we must get you to safety and somewhere you can rest and recover."

Looking at his mother he wondered what all she was keeping secret from him. She stonewalled him every time he asked a question. Now he needed to know what had happened and how to find the murderer of Lesley's parents because of his parents and their desire to keep it quiet.

Finally he could walk no more so he found a secluded spot and sat down and said, "Mom, I think we might need to steal a car. I don't know how much farther I can walk and it's quite a ways to Lesley's house."

Looking at him she said, "Son, I have a plan." As she outlined her plan to him and told him of the car she had hidden at the end of town in her mother's old garage that no-one had ever done anything with but it should still be in perfect running order. Smiling, he said, "Okay, let's go."

Once they got the car he broached the subject with her of what they would do with it once they got to where they were going because somebody was bound to recognize it and start searching for them there.

87

Looking at him like he was dense she told him they'd just leave the keys in it have it running and that cliff near Lesley's house would be a good resting place for that old car. He couldn't believe that she would have thought of that.

While they drove down the dark deserted country roads he hoped they wouldn't meet up with anyone that wanted to harm them. Finally coming to the place where the cliff was he stopped the car. He watched his mother get into the trunk and pull out a suitcase and a briefcase. Looking at her he asked what it was and all she would say was, "Insurance."

As Michael put the rock on the gas pedal he knew as soon as he shifted it into gear it would tumble down the rock cliffs and eventually explode with the gas he and his mother had poured on the seats. Realizing he couldn't move as fast as she could she tapped on his shoulder and stopped him from putting the car into gear and said, "Son, I need to do this for me." Backing off he watched her set it all into motion and knew that there was no turning back.

As they ran into the woods that surrounded the area and began walking towards Lesley's house he knew he wouldn't last much longer and told his mom, "Mom, I think you need to go on ahead and see if someone can come and help me."

Shaking her head no, she said, "Son, I promised myself if it ever came to this I would not leave you behind. We'll stop and rest if we must but we will do this together. Now, we must be quiet so as not to alert anyone to our presence."

As they circled the house he noticed that someone had recently been in the woods and he wondered what they were doing. Before he could figure it out a beefy arm had him and the gruff voice said, "Who are you and why are you here?" Even though he was had by the neck he didn't feel threatened by this person, he actually felt safe, so he said, "I'm Deputy Michael Davids and my mother and I need a safe place to hide and we thought this would be the perfect place."

Turning him around he said, "You did, did ya? Well, as I recall you're the smart aleck officer that arrested Lesley for coming to her home and staying in it. Why you didn't even give her a chance to call someone to get a copy of the deed before you hauled her in and fingerprinted her like a common criminal and you expect her to protect you. Are you crazy, man?"

Hearing their conversation his mother spoke up and said, "Well, I doubt she would do it for him but I think she will do it for me when I tell her what I know about that last evening they were alive and how they helped me and were getting ready to help me leave this area with my son, but, without my husband the sheriff."

"Alright, alright, I understand. We must be quiet. I'll get you into the basement for now and when they wake up you'll need to let them know you are there but do it quietly we think the house might be bugged."

Shaking their heads they both agreed and as he took them into the storm cellar doors they began to wonder what kind of a basement was in this house. As he led them down into the cellar and through a small tunnel they saw a block wall and wondered, what now? Watching the man who hadn't introduce himself yet they saw him touch one brick and the wall moved. As it opened he turned to them and said, "Tell Matt his father let you in."

Walking through the hole in the wall Michael and his Mom couldn't believe it. It was like walking into an upscale hotel with all of the amenities. Hearing the wall close they turned but the man was gone. "Wow" was all he could say as he looked around. This place had a full kitchen, a big living area with several bedrooms and an office downstairs. What was this place and why was it here?

As the mystery deepened he realized how hungry and tired he was and he walked over to the refrigerator and opened it. It was full of food. Relieved he leaned in and grabbed a bottle of water and said to his Mom, "I think I need to rest but I want to check out the office." Walking by her he saw she was opening a suitcase. Suddenly he stopped and said, "Mom, where did you get that? What did you do to get that?"

Looking closely in the suitcase he could see it was full of money. Wads of 20's, 50's and even 100 dollar bills. There had to be thousands of dollars in this suitcase but looking closer he noticed the bills were all aged. The cop came out in him as he looked at his mother with accusation in his voice. "Where did this money come from?"

Closing the suitcase she looked at him and said, "Many years ago it became apparent to me that I was living in a dangerous situation. I started putting money back any time I could from the time you were born until now. This is a result of that. I did it in case I ever had to leave at a moment's notice so that I would be able to start over somewhere with no questions asked. I know right now you are thinking I'm the one who ordered the hit on the preacher and his wife but I had been here that night," pausing she looked at him and saw the coldness in his eyes.

"I never wanted you to know. I never wanted you to find out that your father was a dangerous man to be reckoned with. He's not the man I fell in love with. That man was wonderful and wanted to save the world. He became a policeman because he wanted to help keep people safe and hopefully help deter some from crime. About five years after that he changed. Oh, he tried to be the same man but he was different. He quit coming home on time and when he did he was distracted. I tried to make excuses for him and other than you I had a lot of time on my hands and I met the preacher and his wife. They were such nice people and Lesley was such a cute little girl. You and she played together the night they were killed. We had left and I had forgotten your favorite teddy so we had come back. When we did we got your teddy and on our way out I saw a strange car heading to their house. They saw me. I didn't know it then but they took my license plate number. No they didn't hurt me or you."

Wanting to ask questions but not knowing what to ask or how he just kind of looked at her and said, "Mom, please tell me the rest of the story. I really need to know."

Now was coming the hard part, the part that would destroy what he thought of me, she thought. Continuing, she said, "Let me begin by telling you, I was a young mother who had a gorgeous little boy that I planned on keeping safe no matter what. Please tell me Michael that you understand that, please," she begged him with tears streaming down her face.

91

Not giving him time to answer she continued, "I've kept this secret for over twenty years and now I'm not sure you'll be able to forgive me. No, No, I didn't kill them I never would have. They had shown me what the love of God was all about and what His Spirit could do for me. I was on my way to falling in love with Jesus. I know you don't understand because I was unable to show you. Your father told me if I ever took you to that Pentecostal church he would see to it that I never saw you again. I know, back to what happened that night. By the time we got home your father was there. I was so excited because he was never home early anymore and I thought finally we could have a nice evening together. When I went in it was not only your father but some 'friends' of his. They told me that I was never to go back to that preacher's house or that church. Then I was told if I valued my life and yours I would forget everything I saw tonight. I was then told to put you to bed and to go to bed myself that there was no need for me that night. After putting you to bed I decided to sit by the vent in your bedroom and listen to them talk in the kitchen. I knew those two men that were with your father were the same men I had seen in the car heading to the preacher's house. I heard your father ask them if the job was done and if any witnesses were left. I heard them tell him the little girl had been asleep when they went into the house and that they had chased the preacher and his wife up the stairs. Biting my fist to keep from crying out I heard them tell him that the preacher and his wife were both dead and that the best part of it was the little girl would never find them. I'll never forget that night as long as I live. It has haunted me for years."

Holding his hand up he said, "Mom, I don't know what to say or do so I'm going to go and rest and try to take all of this in. You know we can't keep this a secret anymore and you know we are both targets because you know the whole story that has been buried for years. Somehow I have to figure out how to put all this in perspective about you and Dad."

Walking by her he headed into the bedroom to lay down. Looking up he saw a picture of beautiful West Virginia mountains that said, "I look toward the hills from whence cometh my strength..." Strength, he thought to himself, I have none. Where will I get the strength to get through this. My own father is a common criminal. Closing his eyes he tried not to think about what he had found out.

Sitting on the couch all she could do was cry. Looking up she saw the most beautiful sight she had ever seen. She thought to herself if I didn't know better I'd swear I was seeing an angel. Feeling such sweet peace she looked up and heard this angel looking being say, "Fear not for I am with you."

Turning she saw she was surrounded by these surreal angel looking beings with swords. Looking back to the one that had spoken it spoke again and said, "You are protected, fear not, sleep in peace." Shaking she turned around again and they were all gone but she couldn't get past the sweet peace she felt. She had not felt peace like that in years. She had lived in fear for so long she didn't know what it might feel like to be normal but this had to be close.

Getting up she hid the suitcase in a closet and hung up her clothes. Then feeling very sleepy she went to bed and slept like a lamb. In the next room Michael wondered how his mother had been able to deal with everything that had happened that night. Then he realized that she had loved him enough to put up with it. He didn't know if he would have had the strength to be that strong with a domineering husband. Putting his hands behind his head he felt sleepy and was able to go to sleep without wondering what the morning would bring.

Unexpected Guests

As the house came alive Michael and his mom became aware of noises above them. Knowing she would have to tell her story to Lesley and her friends soon his mother thought it would all go over better with a big breakfast. Before he could get out of bed his mother opened his bedroom door and said, "You're up. Great!" Backing into the room he saw she had a huge tray of food and some medication for him which as he stretched and moved in the bed to get situated he realized he needed it.

Sitting the tray on his bed she began to talk to him as she took a plate for herself and left his on the tray. "Michael, did you know that they have thought of everything. This place is so nice. There is a nice office with a library and even a room off the office that looks like it has an altar and a Bible in it for you to meditate or pray in. I have looked and looked and have been unable to find a way upstairs from down here which is amazing. I wonder why this basement was built this way," pausing he interrupted her and said, "Mom, why are you so excited."

"Son I have something wonderful to tell you that I doubt you'll believe but it made me feel better than I have felt in years and this morning when I got up and found the room with Bible. Well, I just had to go in there and sit down and read some and thank God for bringing us here safely. This is a sanctuary for us. Last night after you went to bed I was sitting on the couch and all I could do was cry. Looking up I saw the most beautiful sight I have ever seen. I felt such sweet peace and then I looked up and heard this angel looking being say, 'Fear not for I am with you.' Turning I saw I was surrounded by these surreal angel looking beings with swords. Looking back to the one that had spoken, it spoke again and said, 'You are protected, fear not, sleep in peace.' When I turned around again they were all gone."

Seeing the look on his face she quickly said, "I know, I know you think I've lost it. Okay, that's a possibility but I don't really think so. I mean think about it. We were able to sneak out of the hospital and you made it to the car I had hidden. That, in and of itself, was a miracle. I believe God knew I needed something I could see to help me get through this and what we have to face with your father and He allowed me to see angels last night."

Hearing someone come down stairs they both looked startled. They could hear a woman singing out of tune but with spirit and freedom knowing whom she worshipped, "I know it was the blood, I know it was the blood, I know it was the blood that saved me. Jesus died upon the cross and I know it was the blood that saved me..." As the singing continued they could hear this lady going back up the stairs and as Michael looked at his mother he saw she was misting up and he said, "Mom what kind of song was she singing, that was interesting."

Looking at him she paused and thought for a moment before she said, "Son, I know I have failed you when it came to your religious education. Please don't hold it against me but after the preacher and his wife were killed I was only allowed to go to your father's church and not to any church that might have some lively worship. I have missed so much over the past twenty years what I just heard. When I would come out here for Bible Studies they would raise their hands and sometimes dance before the Lord."

As Michael's mouth dropped she continued, "I know, I know we've been taught they are all crazy, but they have something. I have felt it and I will not do without it anymore. I really think God has led us here not only to keep us safe but to lead us to a fuller understanding of Him and His ways. If you will just be open enough to listen to them when they explain and watch them when they worship you will see what I mean. Go ahead and be a skeptic for now, but once you feel it, you will understand what I mean."

Michael suddenly felt like he had stepped in the twilight zone. Everything he had ever believed about his parents, about religion, about everything it seemed was seemingly wrong. How would he continue?

As his mother walked over and put her arms around him she said, "Baby, I love you and I have always loved you and I never meant to lead you wrong I just wanted to keep you alive. Now I must figure out how to let those people upstairs know we are here without scaring the daylights out of them."

As they went about their morning routines Lesley realized this was what she had been missing, a family. Success wasn't worth squat if you didn't have anyone to share it with. Hearing Matt's mom go through her morning prayers and singing she had felt so peaceful and happy for the first time in a long time. That was a lot considering she had spent last night not only in her old home but in the bedroom where she had found her parent's murdered. God had really helped her through this.

Matt walked in and said, "My dad left us a note this morning. Seems we have visitors who want people to think they're dead and they have information about your folk's murder. Based on what he said I think this is going to get even more dangerous than it already is. Unfortunately I have to go to town and my mother brought some of Dad's guns with her. She plans to teach you to shoot. I need you to know, Mom's aim has never been the best so when she takes you out I would go where there is nothing she can hit with a bullet that you don't want to replace."

Looking in his twinkling blue eyes she said, "You're kidding, right? I don't believe in weapons of any kind except for war. You want me to be armed? To me that is a horrible thought."

"Lesley, I hate to say this but based on how I feel when I pray we should all be armed because the people who killed your parents have to be very influential and will probably stop at nothing to keep this case from being solved. Do you understand what I'm saying?"

Nodding her head yes she was beginning to realize the seriousness of the situation. As he put his arms around her he said, "Lesley, I will do everything in my power and with the power of God to protect you. By doing that I need you to learn how to shoot even the way my mother shoots. She will at least scare folks off and knowing her accidentally shoot someone if the need arises because I know how bad her aim is. I love her but she can't shoot worth anything."

Very quietly his Mother tapped him on the shoulder and said, "Matt, honey, the least you could do is make sure I'm nowhere in the vicinity when you're talking trash about me and my shooting abilities. Now, I need to know what's going on here. You've got your arms wrapped around Lesley."

"Nothing Mom I was just comforting her."

"Okay, I'll let it go. Now tell me what are we going to do about that note your father left us?"

"Well, I need to leave to visit with folks from the church but before I go we need to go into the secret passageway to the downstairs and meet these folks. I want to make sure you're not in any danger."

"Okay, I realize your father and I are not as young as we used to be but do you really think your father would let anyone near us he thought could be a remote threat let alone a real threat to us. Your father and I are not dense we are actually pretty bright people. I mean we raised you and your sister."

Shaking his head he said, "Okay, I get your point. I may be gone all day because I have to get the church ready for service tomorrow and study for my message. Are you sure you'll be alright?"

He looked questioningly at them and his eyes got as big as saucers as he saw his mother reach down her blouse and pull out a small derringer pistol, then she reached inside her skirt and pulled out a small automatic pistol, not wanting to but wandering as he saw her put those two back and she reached into the back waistband of her skirt and pulled out a switchblade, then she bent down and reached up under the bottom of her skirt and pulled out another small gun.

Smiling she looked at him and Lesley and said, "Now, do you think I am prepared to protect us or not? I have also spent much time in prayer about this situation and I believe God has sent angels to protect us but I know you and your father believe we need to have a means of protection because as you and he say, God expects us to take care of ourselves so we will if we have to But I want you to remember my God is not hard of hearing, nor is His arm short concerning his promises, but to humor you and your father I have these things on me to protect us and I have ammunition stored on me in places I am not letting you see but we are prepared."

As he looked at her he said, "Mama, your faith has always amazed me. I have seen God do things for you, well for us growing up, that I would have never believed if I had not been there so I know God will protect you one way or the other."

"Okay, I'm off to pastor and when I get back tonight I know you all will have tales to tell me of your day. Actually, I can't wait to hear them."

Taking off down the steps he was chuckling under his breath wondering how Lesley would deal with his mother by herself. His mother with him or someone else present was a bit strong but by herself she was downright intimidating. Why he thought they could have made a movie about her and called her the female terminator. Getting in his car to head out he didn't notice how quiet and beautiful it was but yet there was a sinister feel and he felt like he was being watched by someone who wanted to do him harm.

Standing in the woods watching Matt leave was one of the men that had killed Lesley's parents and now had a contract to kill everyone in that house and anyone that was helping them. Rubbing his hands together he thought to himself he could hardly wait until he could get rid of these threats. Even though that kid who thought he was a preacher hadn't preached yet he knew his kind. That kid would get everyone excited at that little church.

Why he remembered Lesley's father and how when they reached a certain number at that church he actually had them help him on that steep roof and had the men of the church tie him up there and he preached from the roof of the church. Before they knew it he had made the front page of all the local papers and even more folks started visiting that little church and bringing their friends.

The more people went to that church the angrier it had made him and the sheriff. They couldn't let some religious nut take over their territory and their money. Why that church even served food to the poor on holidays and sometimes once a month. People loved that kind of thing.

He remembered the businesses donating food and how they had tried to stop it by having the health department check them for citations. Before he had killed that girl's parents he had tried everything to get that preacher to stop from out and out warning him to having him harassed by law enforcement. He still remembered that preacher looking him in the eye and saying, "I know where I will spend eternity and I look forward to it but while I am here I will do the work of God and obey only God when it comes to doing the work of God. He will take care of me and if He, and only He, determines it is my time to go be with Him then it will happen but if not, then He will protect me."

What a freak, he thought to himself. So religious he was stupid when it came to people who tried to explain to him and make him understand why he couldn't preach the way he did. People didn't need this Holy Ghost and speaking in tongues was outright disrespectful for decent folk. Who did he think he was?

Thinking back as he watched the new preacher pull out of the driveway he put his cigarette out stomping it lightly he remembered the night the sheriff snuck up behind that preacher as he came out of the church and grabbed him while other's beat him up. That ole preacher wouldn't quit praying the whole time they were beating him up, actually, now as he recalled he was praying for the ones beating him up. He wasn't even praying for himself. What a nitwit? He hadn't had the brains of a five year old evidently.

Now time to make a plan. As he looked around he didn't notice as he watched the house that he was being watched by one stealthier than he.

Wondering how long this man would stay in the woods and if he would be replaced by someone with even deadlier looking eyes than this guy Lucas wondered what they had gotten into and how dangerous it really was. Watching this guy he knew they needed help. While his wife and son spent so much time in church and prayer he felt like he and God had an agreement, he wouldn't be too mean and he and God would get along just fine as long as he could do what he wanted when he wanted and he didn't have to quit chewing his tobacco.

Noticing action by the house he saw the man watching it go behind a tree. Seeing his wife and Lesley walk out of the house he could see Darlene pointing at the trees but couldn't make out what they were saying. Then he saw Lesley put a couple of bottles on a fence post in the direction of where he was. He knew what was coming and this scared him.

His wife was going to teach someone else to shoot and she couldn't hit the broadside of a barn unless it was moving towards her and then she might miss it. Oh, boy, he needed to get out of their range. He didn't want to get shot by accident. He could care less if that other guy got shot but he didn't want to get shot.

About that time he heard the gun fire and saw a bullet go whizzing by the guy watching the house and then another. As the guy started dancing Lucas almost started laughing but he didn't want to give away his hiding place. Darlene pulled out the automatic and then tried to show off to Lesley by whirling around and shooting.

Now he knew that was too much but he couldn't call out to her and stop her and she knew it. He couldn't risk being seen. He had a feeling she felt someone watching her that shouldn't be and she meant to shoot up the woods and let that person know before they came calling that someone knew how to fire a gun and planned to make sure everyone in the house could do so.

As the bullets started whizzing, he watched the leaves fall since some of her bullets were straying so far off base she was shooting not just the trees but he could see leaves falling with holes in them. It was hilarious watching that guy below him dance while leaves fell like snow on Christmas. Why would people want to kill off good decent folk who just wanted to change lives and make them better? Oh, yes, that's right he thought to himself, they don't want people to change, they want them to stay dependent on drugs and all the other vices.

Man, hiding in a tree was hard on your backside and on your mental abilities. You started thinking about things and what you would do even with bullets whizzing. Right now, he thought I'd like to take out that guy watching the house but all it would do is to cause more people to come and watch the house and cause trouble and he really didn't want that right now.

As he remembered how he had killed the preacher and his wife he now knew some peace since the Sheriffs wife and son weren't a problem anymore. They had found that old car and when they realized it was his wife's mothers. Based on the fact that the mother had passed away a long time ago that the Sheriff's wife was driving it and probably had the son with her and it was at the bottom of the ravine now.

They knew that they had taken that last curve to fast probably thinking they were being followed and then boom, burned to death. Oh, how he wished he had been there to see it or at least to make sure and to see them die. He loved to see people die. To him it was a pleasure.

He wanted to be done with this job he was getting tired of cleaning up messes that should have been dealt with twenty years ago. Why hadn't he listened to the Sheriff when he had told him to make sure he took care of all of the family including the little girl, to leave no witnesses? He thought he hadn't until they were on their way out of there and saw the Sheriff's wife passing them on the road. Man, why hadn't he taken them all out that night and this would have been over with.

When the first bullet whizzed by his ear he thought, nah she can't see me but when the second one caught his pants leg he was ready to hightail it out of the woods but he was stuck where he was at least until they went back into the house. That is if he lived through this experience. When he saw her get out the big automatic rifle he about wet himself.

When she started firing that gun she didn't know how to fire one to two shots at a time it was twenty to thirty at a time. Why that gun should be illegal but it looked like an antique. Bullets started whizzing and he dropped to all fours to hopefully keep out of the range of bullets. He knew he was using up the cat of nine lives that day. Oh, how he wanted to fire back and take care of both of those women right now but he knew if he did the Feds would probably be called in and he couldn't risk that.

So far he had been lucky at not being caught and at having friends within the ranks of the local police department. He was getting older now and knew that soon he would have to stop being the hit man. He had an idea of what he wanted to be but there was someone in the way. That someone would have to go away just like these folks would have to go away. He had noticed that someone else had been in the woods recently and he needed to not only figure out who, but why, and get rid of them. This was going to be a huge cleanup job.

What to do first?

Well, first, he had to hope that woman shooting would run out of ammo soon. No-one would believe him when he told them this story about the forest snowing leaves with holes in them. This job was getting more and more dangerous by the minute.

Originally all he had to worry about was one woman who wanted the case reopened to find her parent's murderer. She had no idea what would happen if it was ever found out how well connected everyone was. They even had people in the FBI and CIA who helped them bring in their product from out of the United States.

Glancing up he saw the younger woman take the gun. If he hadn't known better he would have sworn she could see him. She turned and looked right at him and pulled the trigger firing off three shots at the same time. His hat went flying and she hit it every time. He was in shock. No woman could shoot that well, could they?

Now he knew to finish this off they would need reinforcements and maybe some C-3 or some type of bomb making material. Lying face down in the leaves eating dirt he thought to himself, I'll make her pay. She will pay big time and I will torture her and let her know exactly how and why I killed her parents.

When he saw his wife hand Lesley the gun explaining how to use it he didn't know whether he should be thankful or worried. As he watched Lesley take the gun he noticed that she handled it like a professional. When she shot that man's hat off and then continued to shoot the hat as it bounced with each bullet he wondered just where she had learned to shoot. For someone who evidently didn't like guns she would just about pass a sharpshooter test. Now, he thought to himself, I feel much more comfortable knowing Lesley can hit what she points the gun at and Darlene, well, she would hit things that happened to somehow be in front of her when she fired the gun.

When he saw Lesley turn and look at him he knew he was in trouble and prayed she wouldn't shoot at him. He didn't have on a hat and he didn't have much hair so it wouldn't take much to shoot him out of his perch in the tree. Seeing her aim directly at him he pulled his coat off and hoped it camouflaged exactly where his body was so he wouldn't have any holes in him.

As he felt the bullet hit his jacket he thanked God and his lucky stars that his head hadn't been hit. This girl has been taught by professionals how to shoot he thought to himself. Wonder if anyone has done a background check on her to find out who she is now.

As Lesley fired at the glint in the tree she saw something falling down and prayed she hadn't actually shot anyone. Who knew what four years of military service could do for a small town preacher's daughter including pay for her education She still hadn't lost the touch. That's why in Iraq she had been one of the best sharpshooters and had used her talent to bring down the head of the insurgents in different towns until she had gotten so sick of all the fighting and shooting she had broken down one day in her barracks and had finally prayed.

After that she had finished her tour of duty and when she had come home promptly resigned. Once she had resigned she had gotten her education and found a good church, not that she had gotten into it, she had felt too dirty from all of the killing she had done. She hated it and that's why she hated guns and the situation she had put herself into by coming back here. But she still felt like this must be finished before she could get on with her life. She didn't know how she could ever forgive herself for being a murderer no matter how many awards she had received for doing her "duty". Giving the gun back to Darlene she said, "I'm sorry I need to be alone." She then took off for the house.

Darlene looked at her and wondered what other mystery haunted this beautiful woman. She had researched her once Matt had mentioned her. She knew she was one of the best lawyers in New York and that she fought crime like no-one else. She also knew that people in New York thought that she should run for office but she would not agree to that. She had also learned that Lesley had penned a couple of bestselling books. There was so much to her already and now a new mystery.

What could it be?

A place of Repentance and the Truth

Walking towards her home tears cascading down her face she was thankful for a heritage that even though she hadn't prayed much in her lifetime she knew how and she knew the perfect place to do it. Heading upstairs she went straight to her parent's room. In her mother's walk-in closet there was a door and a place that had been made just to pray. Nothing much was in there but what was, was so important. Opening the door the dust blew out on her. It was very dirty but she didn't care.

She remembered her mother telling her once as a little girl, "Baby when you need to pray go to this room. My Bible will always be here. Find yourself a place with God and let Him change you." Falling to her knees at the altar she buried her head in her mother's Bible and placed the prayer shawl she had kept on the altar around her shoulders. Bowing her head she began to pray and she prayed until she felt power from on high like on the day of Pentecost.

Not knowing how long she had been there she leaned against the wall eyes still shimmering with tears but now they were tears of repentance and thanksgiving for the heritage she had been given. While she still didn't understand all that had happened she now felt so light. It was almost like she could feel her parents with her in this closet. She felt like they knew she had finally come home to Jesus.

While outside Darlene was getting worried. She had continued to practice shooting. She just felt like someone was watching that shouldn't be. She prayed she didn't hit her husband. She knew she'd hear about shooting up the woods but it had to be done. Somebody had to give these people a message that they were not going to take this sitting down. While she believed God could and would protect them she also believed in being prepared for any problem that might arise.

As she headed into the house she could hear someone singing and it sounded like they were singing in tongues. What on earth, she thought to herself, who could be here praying like that? Following the noise it led her to the Master bedroom. Walking in, it was stronger so she followed the noise to the closets and saw an opening she had not noticed before. Then she saw Lesley leaning against the wall her face wet with tears but glowing with the presence of the almighty God and King.

Knowing how protective she felt, herself, about this young lady after only two days she wanted to rejoice, dance, and scream in happiness but she didn't want to scare her so she left her and went to the room she was staying in. She began thanking God for what He was doing through this situation.

When she finished she knew they needed to figure out how to get into the basement from inside the house. She hoped her husband had managed to come into the house because knowing him he already had it figured out. As she entered the kitchen she saw the love of her life sitting on the stool. How she loved that blue eyed, reddish looking half bald man with his handlebar mustache. Relaxing in his arms she said breathlessly, "I love you."

Looking at her he said, "Babe, I love you too but if you ever try to shoot me out of a tree again I have news for you if I get out alive, I'll skin you alive."

Kissing him fully on the mouth she said, "Really..."

"Ummm, kiss me again like that, I seem to have forgotten what I was upset about..."

Laughing she said, "I thought so.."

Laying her head on his shoulder she said, "I take it when I was teaching, let me rephrase that, thought I was teaching Lesley to shoot I didn't hit you."

"No, you didn't hit me but you did put a bullet through my jacket."

As her face turned white she said, "Oh, I'm so sorry, so sorry but I felt like someone was watching us that I needed to let know we were serious about defending ourselves."

Looking at her he said, "Baby someone was watching you because I was watching him. When those leaves started falling like snowflakes because of the holes being shot in them I wanted to laugh but I couldn't. I watched that man dance and it was hilarious. He's older but babe, this is so much more serious than we originally thought. The man in the woods has dead eyes. He's been doing this a while. He intends to leave no witnesses. I know that look."

"Oh, John, what are we to do?"

"I believe it's one of your favorite things to do. Pray and trust God to protect all of us."

Nodding her head she then went for a piece of paper and wrote on it asking, "Has the house been swept yet?"

He shook his head yes and said, "No bugs remain."

"How then do we get to our guests?"

He responded, "Come and I'll show you."

Opening the pantry he pushed one side and it opened. She saw a door and he opened it. There was a stairwell and at the end a brick wall. Looking questioningly at him, he opened a panel on the side and punched in a code. The brick wall slid across and it was open.

"Wow," she said, "How on earth did you figure out how this worked."

"We talked to Lesley's grandparents. They knew the lives of their kids had been threatened and he helped build this. No-one else knows about it in the family or the community."

Hearing the door slide open Michael immediately jumped to his feet still clad in a hospital gown because he had no clothes with him stood ready to battle but knew he was woefully under armed waited hoping that these were friends coming through the door. Grinning as she walked through the door, Darlene said, "I see you had to check out of the hospital in a hurry?"

"Yes, Ma'am I did. Who are you?"

"Why I'm Darlene and he's my husband, George. We're here to help Lesley who I believe you arrested."

As they shook hands and got acquainted Darlene knew they needed to get Matt some clothes. Thankful that her husband had some medical training he checked the wound on Michael's arm. It was a through and through so it only needed to heal. They had been able to stitch it back up. Just keeping it bandaged and antibiotics would take care of it. George and Darlene had family in the area that had doctors about an hour away so he knew he could get antibiotics for Michael. He also knew he'd be making a trip for some clothes for this big guy. None of his would work, he was only 5' 10" and this guy must be well over six foot.

Michael introduced his mom to Darlene as, "This is my mother Ella. She's the only witness that can make a positive identification of the murderers of Lesley's parents and the car they were driving that night."

Darlene gasped and said, "Stop right there. We need you to tell this to Lesley. Let me go get her."

As they waited George talked to Michael and Ella trying to figure out how this was coming together so fast. When they explained Michael had gotten shot and then an attempt made on his life at the hospital as a warning Michael said, "Mom decided we weren't taking a chance on them somehow killing me the third time and then coming after her. She felt like this would be the safest place for us to be because they would never suspect it."

George nodded his head and then heard Lesley and Darlene coming. Darlene had warned Lesley about the Deputy being in his hospital gown but when she saw him like that all she could do was laugh. When she finally got done Matt said, "I'm so glad I was able to provide you with some amusement today."

Grinning she replied, "After our first meeting it really makes my day to see you in a dress." Then she soberly continued, "I'm sorry you're hurt and that somehow I've gotten you mixed up in my mess. You don't have to worry about anything you'll be safe here."

Looking at Lesley Michael said, "There's something you need to know about 'your mess' as you call it. My mother and your parents were friends. She has something she needs to tell you but before she starts I want you to realize how much danger she's been in and why she's been quiet all these years. Her life and mine as a child was threatened by the people who took out your parents."

Stunned Lesley tried to remain calm but looked directly at Ella and said in an authoritative voice, "Someone please go on."

Ella got up and came over to her and sat down beside her on the sofa, saying, "Sweetie, your parents were wonderful people. They taught me Bible studies and helped me see that what they had was real. They helped me find it for myself along with so many others. One night I was to come out here for a Bible Study. You see I needed extra time with them because of my situation. So after we got done I left and headed home but on my way home I passed a car coming down the road. Since this is the last house there's no doubt where they were going. It was dusk and I recognized the two men driving as some of my husband's friends. When I got home I put Matt to bed and about an hour later my husband came and got me. He told me that I had to forget anything I saw that night otherwise they would hurt Matt and me."

Pausing she looked at Lesley who was sitting stone faced. She was wondering what kind of response she would get. So she continued, "After I was duly threatened I snuck out of the house and came over here. I found you outside standing by the back door covered in blood. I knew I couldn't take you home and I knew you weren't safe in the house or near here so I took you to the woods and told you to hide until you heard your grandparent's calling you. Thankfully it was a warm night so I knew you'd be fine in your robe and slippers. I hated leaving you like that but I had no choice."

Darlene couldn't believe the story she'd just heard so she looked at Ella and said, "Really, there was nowhere you could have taken her. Like maybe to her grandparents?"

"You still don't understand. If it had come out that I had come back here somehow they would have tried me for the murder. My husband was so mad that I had been out here that night. You see, prior to this he had told me I could not go to any Bible studies or to church so I would come over here for a get together which just

119

happened to be a Bible study. That night Lesley's parents were helping me make plans to leave my husband and disappear. He was the Sherriff back then and he's the Sherriff to this day. He has connections high up so anything he wants done gets done. They and I knew that. I'm afraid I'm partially to blame for them being killed. At the time I didn't know this but by learning how to listen in on conversations I wasn't supposed to hear I found out that my husband was the head of the local mafia."

Michael looked at his mother like she had dropped in from another planet with questions and anger in his eyes.

"Mom, why didn't you ever tell me any of this?"

Realizing she was about to lose her son forever if she couldn't explain this to his satisfaction she said, "Son, I couldn't. Your father not only threatened me but he threatened you. I couldn't allow anything to happen to you. You were the best thing that ever happened to me. When I met and married your father I had no idea he was like this. I was young and naïve. I wanted to believe the best in everyone. Until you came along I didn't worry and then he didn't just beat me he was starting in on you. I was scared. I had to do everything I could to protect you from him. When I found Jesus I felt like my life was starting over and then Lesley's parents were killed."

Looking at her no-one could believe the story she had just told them but finally Michael said, "Mom, I need time to digest all of this. I just can't quite believe all of it. I knew Dad was somehow involved but I don't ever remember him hurting me or you and if that's not true maybe some of this other stuff you just told us isn't true also."

Leaning her head back she said, "Well, there's something else you need to know that I haven't told you yet. You see your Dad wasn't quite as safe with everything as he thought he was so I managed to get some copies of some records that he had with names of some very high ranking people. Call it my insurance policy. I made sure to go to another town and get a safety deposit box and mail a letter to my friend who lives in California giving her the key to the safety deposit box and telling her that if anything ever happened to me more than likely it was murder no matter what anyone said. I also told her to get this information out of this state and to the media where it would be at least given a trial and bring some much needed spotlight on this county. When that was done I took another copy to your Dad and let him know I had it. As he had me by the hair of the head slamming me against the wall I told him that if he killed me it would be all over the news within a few days and that if I disappeared the same thing would happen. Needless to say that night the beatings stopped. We've had sort of a truce since then."

Lesley didn't know what to say to all she'd been told. She didn't want to embrace this woman but she didn't want to walk away like everything she'd been told meant nothing because it did mean something. So she excused herself telling them she needed some time to think she went upstairs to spend some time alone and think about everything.

The story was so shocking but it was believable. Could this actually be a whole lot bigger than her parents? If it was, what role would she play in finding their killers?

The Plan and The Angels

While there was a lot she didn't understand what she did understand was that this was much more dangerous than she had ever imagined. She had no idea what should be done next. She knew everyone in that room had a death warrant hanging over their head. Now she needed to call in her personal favors and get protection for all of them. She had contacts and she knew how to use them. It sounded like it was time to make a plan.

Sitting in the living room looking out the French doors it looked so peaceful. How ironic? Peace? Not here. Trouble and turmoil that's what she was in the middle of. That sounded like an old gospel song. One her parents had probably no doubt sung to her. Walking over to the big cherry desk her father had placed in the family room because when he studied he wanted to be available to his baby girl. She remembered fondly other pastors asking him, "How do you study with a child underfoot?"

And his reply always made her smile, "She's our blessing from God. How would I study without her near. I want her to understand what we believe. If I'm always behind closed doors she'll never understand the power of God or how long it takes to get a message ready for church."

Wow, being here was bringing back all kinds of memories. Sitting down at the desk she opened it to look for a pen and was shocked to find a message in her father's handwriting half written in the desk. She could hardly believe the title of the message and here she was some twenty years later to write a plan.

The Plan of Salvation

Most people don't know how to come to God. Most don't understand sin. In this day and age it seems that everything is accepted. There is no sin. We are under grace but my Bible tells me in Romans 3:23-24; "For all have sinned and come short of the glory of God; Being justified freely by His grace through the redemption that is in Christ Jesus: Whom God hath set forth to be a propitiation through faith in His blood, to declare His righteousness for the remission of sins that are past, through the forbearance of God; To declare I say at this time His righteousness: that He might be just, and the justifier of him which believeth in Jesus."

So we have all sinned, but Jesus is our propitiation. That means He is our atoning sacrifice. He died so that we might have life and have it more abundantly. I hear ministers saying we live under grace. Anything goes. My Bible does not tell me that. It also tells me in Romans 6:1-7; "What shall we say then? Shall we continue in sin that grace may abound? God forbid. How shall we that are dead to sin live any longer therein? Know ye not, that so many of us as were baptized into Jesus Christ were baptized into His death? Therefore we are buried with Him by baptism into death: that like as Jesus Christ was raised up from the dead by the glory of the Father, even so we also should walk in newness of life. For if we have been planted together in the likeness of His death we shall be also in the likeness of His resurrection: Knowing this, that our old man is crucified with Him, that the body of sin might be destroyed, that henceforth we should not serve sin. For he that is dead is freed from sin?"

Let's discuss this passage. The Bible tells us we should not continue in sin just so grace may abound. Yes, we're covered by grace but once we come to Jesus and are baptized we are a new man and no longer serve sin. We are free from sin. Sin is to be destroyed. Has that happened in your life? If not, let's talk about how to destroy sin.

Acts 2:38 says, "Then Peter said unto them, Repent, and be baptized every one of you in the name of Jesus Christ for the remission of sins, and ye shall receive the gift of the Holy Ghost."

So in order to get rid of sin you need to repent. This is not pleasant. It requires you to ask forgiveness from God for what you've done. Then you need to turn away from the sin and do it no longer. If you've done something and you need to go talk to someone and ask their forgiveness you need to do that. Then it requires baptism by full body immersion in water with a minister calling over you in the name of Jesus. This is where you identify with His resurrection and you are picking up your cross to follow Him. After this, because of your obedience you'll be filled with the gift of the Holy Ghost of which the outward sign is speaking in other tongues. You say, this can't still be happening today? Most definitely it still happens and it needs to happen to you.

You say my Bible tells me in John 3:16, "For God so loved the world that He gave His only begotten son, that whosoever believeth in Him should not perish but have everlasting life." What you forget is that same Bible says in James 2:19, "Thou believest that there is one God; thou doest well: the devils also believe, and tremble."

So, I ask you, do you think devils will be in heaven?

As the ink rolled across the page into an indecipherable scribble she realized her father must have been working on this the night they were murdered. Not realizing she was crying but seeing spots appearing on the paper she quickly moved it and put it back in the drawer.

Thinking about her father's message she knew she needed to pray until she felt that power again like she had earlier today. She remembered being in church and feeling God touch her and her speaking in a heavenly language. All of her psychiatrists had told her it was a blessing her parents had died so she wasn't raised in a pastor's home. Her psychiatrist had said that the childhood trauma of seeing her parent's dead was less traumatic than what a pastor's child would go through. Shaking her head she thought that psychiatrist must be missing parts of her brain.

But as her father's message said in this day and age everything appears to be ok, there is no sin. Wow, if he had lived to today when so much is accepted he would really be preaching hard, or would he? She had been in some churches where it seemed everything was wonderful. All the pastor's talked about was love, joy and peace. No matter what you did or hadn't done you were ok.

That's when she had quit going. She had felt something was missing. She wanted old time church like when her folks were alive. She wanted someone to tell her like her father's message had that all had sinned. She needed someone to make her uncomfortable with the way she was living. She wanted someone to tell her she needed to take up her cross and follow Jesus.

Why couldn't she find that again?

Searching now for some blank paper to figure out how to protect everyone involved she started making notes of those she needed to contact. Unfortunately with all the links the local people have she felt that she would have to leave in order to use a phone somewhere else where no-one would know she was at. Where could she go that she would be safe in order to coordinate what was needed.

Who would have thought her life would become this twisted with intrigue and the mafia. She had never really thought that was the problem. She knew if certain people came around her all she could do was scream as a child after the murders. That was one of the reasons her grandparents decided to leave the area. They had been told to get her under control period. No excuses or she would be the next victim. So to save her life they left.

Looking down at her list she heard the front door open and saw Matt walking towards her. He is so handsome, she thought to herself. I could really get lost in those baby blue eyes. Shaking herself mentally, she told herself, not now. You have to focus or you and others will die.

Matt looked at her and wondered at her odd reaction. At first he thought she was glad to see him and then it was almost like she changed right in front of him from sincere happiness to cold and aloof. Not knowing what was going on he decided to play it cool and said, "So what's up?"

"Check out this list of things I think we need to help us on this project." Even though they said the house was clear of any listening devices she still wasn't taking any chances. Nodding his head that he understood he looked at the list.

1. Contact my special forces friends to come and help.
2. Contact the director of the FBI and the CIA.
3. Have someone bring some dynamite.
4. Hire a security agency with access to more specialized weaponry.
5. Stockpile food, water, armor, and ammunition.
6. Prepare for a siege.
7. Sharpshooters posted throughout the property.

Looking at her after reading this list he wondered just who she was. She had said she didn't like weapons and here on this list was ways and means to get even more weapons.

Seeing the questions in his eyes she spoke hoping that someone was listening, "I served in the military for four years. I was in special forces so I have training that most

128

don't even hear about and I can't discuss but suffice it to say I am able to take care of myself. However, there are many of us in danger now. I will protect what is mine and those who have stuck their necks out for me."

About that time she heard a shot fired. Grabbing him, down they went behind the desk, as glass exploded around them. Suddenly the stakes had gotten much higher. Praying that everyone else was downstairs she knew they were a sitting duck and something had to be done and fast. Running for her bedroom with him following yelling, "It's too dangerous!"

She said, "It's too dangerous not to." He didn't know it but she had a satellite phone and all she needed to do was punch in a code. They would trace her location and a team would be set in motion to come within hours. She only hoped they could survive that long. If she was lucky what had just happened was just a scare tactic for now to put them on edge.

Grabbing her briefcase she pulled out her satellite phone and punched in the code. She had thought she'd never have to use it but because her special forces group had been so elite this was one of their perks. They had one group that was after each of them so they knew they might at some point need each other's protection.

Watching them run he laughed with sinister glee. Talking to himself he said, "I'll have them so unnerved by the time I kill them they'll be begging me to do it." As he watched the house he saw lights going and then watched them attempting to fix the window. Didn't they know that wouldn't stop him if he wanted in.

Chuckling he decided to go get some rest and get ready for the next siege. One someone would die in. Hopefully it would be one of those women that had been shooting earlier.

Looking at her punch in this code she grabbed a pen and paper and wrote on it.

"The stakes just got a lot higher. You need to go check on your folks. I have a lot of friends in high places. People will be coming tomorrow with everything we need so if the roads are impassable like I think they might be we won't need to leave. I would not get in a car and try to leave. They're probably booby trapped. We need to stay in the house tonight. Lights need to go on and off. Somehow we need to make the downstairs secure. I know that was a large plate glass window but there has to be something we could use to cover it. We've got to get all these windows covered so they can't tell what is going on."

Nodding his head he pointed downstairs and mouthed let's go, after grabbing clothes. So they grabbed clothes for his folks and themselves and headed downstairs. They were flipping lights on and off as they went. He was also looking for something that could be used to secure the window that was now very insecure. Finally in the mud room he found an old piece of plywood that looked like it had been one of Lesley's art projects. He looked at her and said, "Can we use this?"

She replied, "We don't have a choice."

Grabbing a hammer and nails she followed him, checking out every nook and cranny to make sure they didn't have any unwanted visitors until they got to the window where they nailed it in place.

Knowing they were being watched they did what they had to do quickly and quietly. Then they bumped and made noise going back upstairs so it would look like they were going to bed flipping lights off and on. Once the lights were off they felt their way tiptoeing to the kitchen and went into the pantry shutting the door lightly.

As they pushed the one side of the pantry and headed downstairs she realized the downstairs was a safe room, actually a safe house. Because if you didn't know it was there you wouldn't know. When that brick wall slid across after they got into the basement she knew they were secure then she crumbled like a deck of cards being shuffled when they fly out of a person's hands.

Matt had gone on ahead and when he saw her crumble he dropped what he was carrying went to her on the floor and cradled her in his arms. Carrying her he began to pray for her soul, for her mental health, for her physical health, for protection and strength in the days ahead. He began to remind God of the times in the Bible where angels had surrounded and protected people. One story that came to mind was II Kings 6:15-18;

> *"And when the servant of the man of God was risen early, and gone forth, behold an host compassed the city both with horses and chariots. And his servant said unto him, Alas, my master! How shall we do? And he answered, Fear not: for they that be with us are more than they that be with them. And Elisha prayed, and said, Lord, I pray thee, open his eyes that he*

may see. And the Lord opened the eyes of the young man; and he saw: and, behold, the mountain was full of horses and chariots of fire round about Elisha. And when they came down to him, Elisha prayed unto the Lord, and said, Smite this people, I pray thee, with blindness. And he smote them with blindness according to the word of Elisha."

As she came to he couldn't resist. He pressed a kiss to her forehead. Knowing she was starting back spiritually he knew he couldn't even consider a relationship with her yet but if she continued her journey back then one day. It would be a while but one day, Lord willing, this woman might be his wife.

Even though it was late he knew once everyone heard what happened upstairs that they would need a Bible study and to pray. God had given him the perfect passage to share to encourage them tonight.

As they brought everyone up to date on what happened Michael had the best sense of humor and said, "So I guess I need to get used to wearing this hospital gown for now."

As they all laughed heads were nodded that yes, that's what Michael would have to do. Since he was still recovering and needed to rest that would be fine. As they got comfortable Matt started quoting the scripture in II Kings 6 reminding all of them of the mighty things God could and would do for His people if they would only pray. So after he reminded them he then told them to stand and hold hands and pray fervently like they might die tomorrow because it was very possible if God didn't intervene and Lesley's 911 to her special forces friends didn't get the desired result.

While they were praying they felt a breeze and when they opened their eyes they could see a host of angels behind each one of them all dressed in sparkling robes of white with flaming swords. As they all fell to their knees they began to thank God for allowing them to see this heavenly host encamped round about them.

After this it was hard to want to go to bed but they knew they needed rest to prepare for what tomorrow might bring. So everyone had to double up because downstairs was only three bedrooms, two bathrooms, a family room and a kitchen. It was decided that Matt's parents would get a bedroom, Matt and Michael would share a room with Lesley and Ella sharing a room.

The Apology, Angels, and Special Forces Details

Ella looked at Lesley when they went into their room and said, "Lesley, I'm so sorry it took me so long to come forward and tell what happened."

Turning slowly around to face Ella, Lesley responded, "You know today when you told all that happened I wasn't ready to hear why someone hadn't come forward. I wanted to hurt not only the people that did that to my parents but I wanted to hurt anyone that knew anything about it and didn't help me. I feel like I've been held hostage by this all these years. The memories have haunted me. I've wondered why? Why couldn't I remember? If I loved my parents I should be able to remember and bring their killers to justice. You've held the key all along. I truly was asleep when it all happened and never knew it until today. Everyone always thought I was just blocking it out, but I wasn't. I didn't want to understand why you didn't come forward. I didn't want to feel your pain but I do."

Pausing and seeing that Ella wanted to say something she put up her hand and said, "Let me finish. But after hearing what you had to say about it and why you did what you did. After listening to you I took some time by myself. I had to think about it. I don't know what I would have done had I been in your shoes. I really don't know if I would have done anything any differently. I see your tears and I feel mine coursing down my cheeks once again like rivers. I need to forgive you not just for you but for me because I understand. You need to know this too. Ever since I became an adult I haven't been in church. I've gone just to keep up appearances and keep everyone off my back but my heart wasn't in it. Well, I found a place of repentance just a little while ago. I know that God will protect us. He didn't bring all of this far to leave us."

Smiling through the tears she continued, "Now that sounds like something my parents would have said to you at some point. You do understand what I mean. Let's move on and figure out how to stay alive and support each other through this mess. God will not let us down. After hearing Matt's Bible study and seeing those angels surrounding us. I think if I was the people trying to kill us I'd be scared tonight but I feel like we're all going to sleep like babies knowing those angels are keeping watch over us."

Ella could hardly speak after hearing Lesley so eloquently accept what she had told them much earlier that day. She just walked over to Lesley and hugged her. As they wept they bonded. Ella thought to herself, I hope I'm blessed to get to help mother your daughter,

Amanda. You did so much for me I want to help do this for you. I want to give back to you what you did for me over twenty years ago.

As all the lights went off in the basement that no-one knew was there, a host of angels encamped round about the house watching those who were watching the folks they were protecting.

As the old man who had broken the window walked out one angel picked up his sword to kill him when an older wiser angel stopped him and said, "It is not time yet, soon, but not yet."

The younger angel looked at him and said, "Why not now? We could end this for them tonight. Why do they have to suffer? Why should they be afraid? Why do others need to be called in when we're here and we can do the job?"

The older angel looked at him and said, "It is not for us to say when we will do what we will do but for God to give us our orders. For now, our orders are to wait. There are some other things that must happen first. God has given us orders. We will obey our orders."

During the night the other thirteen members around the world of Lesley's special ops team had received the message and corresponded with each other. In her second message she had told them everything they needed and that they were holed up in a safe area but they had no idea how unsafe the outside was at this time.

As they gathered items together they knew it would take 24 hours to get there. They needed to arrive under the cloak of darkness with no fanfare so no-one would know they had arrived. They were legally trained killers. They would secure the area and rescue the hostages no matter the cost. Even though they weren't being held at gunpoint they were hostages so that helped them to understand the types of weapons and explosive devices they needed to bring with them.

Lesley had been trained well. She had given them her coordinates and they were able to look it up on the internet. Thanks to the access they had to spy satellites above America, well, actually the whole world. They were able to take it down to street level and see the terrain of the mountainous area. It looked like a quiet sleepy little town where you would want your family to grow up. However, a sinister presence was there and needed to be taken out.

Lesley had also sent an encrypted email to each member of her old team telling them what had happened to her parents and why. She also let them know they were dealing with a local mafia that had links with the FBI and CIA. This told them that no one could know about this mission until it was successful. This team had that kind of clout. They were paid well but had to be completely independent of any authority except the President of the United States.

As they loaded up their vehicles to catch private planes to rendezvous in Washington D.C. because the team had gone many different places when they weren't on assignment some had to come from far flung places like India, Pakistan, and the Caribbean while some were in the Midwest. They each had contacts that were meeting them in D.C. with supplies they could not get where they were at or where they were going.

A private plane had been chartered to take them to Morgantown, West Virginia where in the dead of night a Hummer would be waiting. Electric blue with tinted windows just like the one Lesley had rented so if anyone saw it out they would think she was out. One of the guys had even gotten a red wig so that he would look like her. Everything was meticulously planned and well thought out.

As each member of the special force team left their families for this assignment from one of their own. They kissed their family members who could not be told where they were going, why, or even if they'd be notified if they never came home. This is called living on the edge. Some family members were questioning why they're loved ones were doing this especially the ones that were no longer in the military. All they would say was, "I've been deployed for a special mission. I'll be back soon."

Most don't know that we have teams who literally give their all to keep us safe but their families also give their all.

One man kissed his wife and each of his three sleeping children. While a different one held his newborn son for the first time. As he handed the baby to his wife he kissed her and told her he loved her and would be back as soon as he could. Another on his honeymoon knew his bride would not understand but Lesley had saved his life once during a firefight so this was a no brainer. He had to go. He hoped someday his bride could forgive him for leaving her on their honeymoon. He had told her from the beginning due to being in the special

139

forces it didn't matter what was planned he could be deployed at a moment's notice and due to the type of special forces they were in even after retirement they could be called back up at a moment's notice.

The oath they had taken to be a part of this most elite group was secretive but they were trained to do what others could not and would not do. Each of them had blood on their hands from those that had killed some in hand-to-hand combat, some with explosive devices and others as sharp shooters.

Each one of them was dressed all in black from head to toe. Everything had to just blend in during the night. While they were preparing around the world in Morgantown someone else was picking up all the supplies in that electric blue hummer. It was being loaded full with everything they would need that wasn't being brought with them. With the right amount of money and/or friends anything can be done quickly.

In this sleepy little town there was one house where everyone was up all night. Even though his wife and son had supposedly been killed, the local Sherriff who was the head of the local mafia was pulling in all his favors to find out what was going on at the house. He knew they had guns. He also knew the community would have a fit if he rushed in there and said they were breaking the law. This has to be done with the mafia and his help from the FBI and CIA.

He had all of his people ready to roll at a moment's notice. Different ones were already hiding out in the woods to see what was going on. What they were reporting back to him was strange. They were saying they couldn't see anything because the fog was so thick around the house. What was funny is, it wasn't foggy anywhere else. How do you explain that?

He knew if his wife and son weren't dead when he found them they would be. He was over it. He didn't care what she had on him anymore, enough was enough. Then he finds out that his chief person had gone out there to scare them by firing a gun through one of the plate glass windows.

What was that man thinking? Now they were on guard. That was the last thing he wanted. He had wanted the element of surprise but now it was gone. Scratching his head he looked around at his team sitting at the dining room table and said, "Men, we've got to go in there with the mentality that we will be the only survivors. Every one of them must be killed. I don't care if they are my family or yours. They must die!"

Banging his fist on the table and seeing everyone nod in agreement he knew he had them with him. Now he had to plan how to attack in one fell swoop to gain the upper hand so that they would come out the winner. As his team left he let them know that tomorrow he'd have a plan of attack. Sitting back down at the table he began to plan and make calls. He knew he needed explosives so that he could blow up any and all evidence along with the people involved.

A lot of people would die in a few days including his own but they couldn't know he was planning their demise. He knew once this all unfolded even his contacts at the FBI and CIA couldn't keep out the investigation that would follow so he had to make sure that anyone with inside knowledge no longer lived except him and a few others who were new to the group and didn't know the details from all those years ago.

"I will not go to prison!"

Looking around he realized he had screamed to no-one. Realizing he was alone he needed to get a grip. He was losing it. Right now he needed to be more together than he'd ever been before because he was about to start the fight of his life for his life.

Preparation for Battle and finding God

Stretching Lesley realized she had slept and felt refreshed but she had dreamed of her parents. In the dream they were talking to her. She closed her eyes to try to capture it one more time but it was going away.

"Don't leave me," she screamed at them in the dream.

In the dream her father replied, "Lesley, I have to go but remember it says in God's Word in II Chronicles 20:15 '…Be not afraid nor dismayed by reason of this great multitude; for the battle is not yours, but God's.' Lesley, you need to finish getting right with God before this battle. You have to forgive those that killed us before you will truly be right with God. You've felt God's presence earlier today and the Holy Ghost has filled you but you have this one last thing you must do. You've been away a long time but Jesus is waiting on you to come to Him. Talk to Matt, he will help you. We must go now, but remember, this battle belongs to God!"

Opening her eyes, her face wet with tears she realized she must have slept longer than anyone else because she could hear them up. She knew she needed a few minutes to digest the latter part of the dream. She knew in her dream she had walked and talked with her parents. They had hugged her and prayed for her but now in preparation for the battle to come she needed to not only have a strategy for the battle but a strategy for her soul.

Matt, his folks, Michael (still in the hospital gown) and Ella were all gathered around the table trying to figure out how to come out on top when Lesley came in the room. Walking in she said, "I have a plan."

"First of all, let me tell you about a dream I had." Seeing the questions in their eyes she raised her hand and continued, "Please let me tell you the dream and then we can discuss it. I dreamed last night I was with my parents. In this dream I walked and talked with them for a long time. While I have called in people to help us who are very well trained to fight to the death God let me know this battle will be long over before they arrive tomorrow night. I saw when I was walking and talking with my parents legions of angels all around this home and it enveloped in a thick dense fog while everywhere else there is no fog. I saw that the fog is the angels circling this property. So far all they are doing is watching but God wants the glory for this battle. I can't believe I'm saying this it's so far out of my league. My parents told me I needed to get right with God before the battle starts. They told me I have to forgive the people that killed them. I feel like if I need to get right with God so do all of us. They also told me

Matt would have the answers we would need. So, I guess, after we eat we need a Bible Study and prayer meeting. I'm not sure of the terminology but you know what I mean."

Matt looked at her and said, "Let's eat and then we'll go in the other room where we can be comfortable and I'll give a mini Bible lesson hopefully we'll get through before the bullets start flying."

Outside the house, the Sherriff, the men that worked with him, and the folks that had flown in from the FBI and CIA who were part of the mafia could not figure out why there was so much fog around one property in the area. They were trying to figure out if it was some new weapon that was being tried out to see how well it worked.

In the meantime they were going on in through the woods and getting set up to blow everything to smithereens if they were unable to get them to come out on their own. If they came out on their own it would be a death sentence. Everyone had been told to shoot to kill, no exceptions.

As they all found seats in the living room of the basement, Matt said, "You're not going to believe this but today is Sunday. I think we need to go to the church. I feel like God will protect us. It starts in an hour. But first let's go upstairs where we have more room and an altar because the message God has given me for this morning is not the one I need to share with all of you right now."

147

Once they all got settled upstairs he opened his Bible and said, "First I'm going to give you a little history and then share the plan of salvation with you. In Genesis 1:1 it says, *'In the beginning God created the heaven and the earth:'* then in Deuteronomy 6:4 the Bible says, *'Hear O Israel: the Lord our God is one Lord:'* Now let's go to Isaiah 9:6-7 where it is prophesied about Jesus, *'For unto us a child is born, unto us a son is given: and the government shall be upon his shoulder: and his name shall be called Wonderful, Counsellor, The mighty God, The everlasting Father, the Prince of Peace. Of the increase of His government and peace there shall be no end, upon the throne of David and upon his kingdom, to order it and to establish it with judgment and with justice from henceforth even for ever. The zeal of the Lord of hosts will perform this.'* Any questions so far?"

Looking around he saw them shaking their heads no so he continued, "I know I'm going through this rather fast but we don't have the privilege of a lot of time. I feel God wants y'all to get right with him quickly so I'm taking you through the Bible and a few prophecies so you'll understand the plan of salvation. Then we'll pray, you'll repent, be baptized in Jesus name in the bathtub and God will give you the gift of the Holy Ghost. But I've gotten ahead of myself back to the Bible. Let's look at Joel 2:28-29 where it says, *'And it shall come to pass afterward that I will pour out my spirit upon all flesh; and your sons and your daughters shall prophesy, your old men shall dream dreams, your young men shall see visions: And also upon the servants and the handmaids in those days will I pour out my spirit.'*"

Pausing Matt couldn't hardly believe he was teaching a home Bible study in the midst of artillery being lined up all around a home. Knowing they were being watched he picked his Bible back up and quickly thumbed to Matthew and said, "Before I read this let me remind you that Joseph and Mary were engaged. They were not married and she was a virgin when she was found pregnant and had told Joseph. This is where I'm starting to read Matthew 1:19-25, *'Then Joseph her husband, being a just man, and not willing to make her a publick example, was minded to put her away privily. But while he thought on these things, behold, the angel of the Lord appeared unto him in a dream, saying, Joseph, thou son of David, fear not to take unto thee Mary thy wife: for that which is conceived in her is of the Holy Ghost. And she shall bring forth a son, and thou shalt call his name Jesus: for he shall save his people from their sins. Now all this was done, that it might be fulfilled which was spoken of the Lord by the prophet, saying, Behold a virgin shall be with child, and shall bring forth a son, and they shall call his name Emmanuel, which being interpreted is, God with us. Then Joseph being raised from sleep did as the angel of the Lord had bidden him, and took unto him his wife: And knew her not til she had brought forth her firstborn son: and he called his name JESUS.'"*

Knowing this was a lot of information he was giving them fast he paused and said, "Are y'all with me so far? I don't really have time to explain a lot so you're going to have to take the Bible literally, word for word so we can get to the praying. So now let's go to John 1:1-5, *'In the beginning was the Word, and the Word was with God, and the Word was God. The same was in the beginning with God. All things were made by Him: and without Him was not any thing made that was made. In him was life; and the life was the light of men. And the light shineth in darkness; and the darkness comprehended it not.'* Now we'll skip down to verse 14 in this same chapter where it says, *'And the Word was made flesh, and dwelt among us,(and we beheld His glory, the glory as of the only begotten of the Father,) full of grace and truth.'"*

Taking a breath he said, "Now I'm going to go to John 3:16 where it says, *'For God so loved the world that He gave His only begotten son that whosoever believeth in Him should not perish but have everlasting life.'* Now I know that some of you in this room think that believing on Jesus is enough and I have a question for you. If that is enough why does the Bible say in James 2:19, "*Thou believest that there is one God: thou doest well: the devils also believe, and tremble.'* Even though we're short on time I want to take a minute here and see if you have any questions. Before you start let me ask you this, If the devil believes and trembles will he be in heaven?"

As he looked around he knew Michael and his mother were thinking. Lesley had a foundation so he didn't really expect any questions from her. Hearing only silence he cleared his throat and said, "Okay, now let's go to Matthew 28:19 where Jesus is talking and says, *'Go ye therefore, and teach all nations, baptizing them in the name of the Father, and of the Son, and of the Holy Ghost:'* I want you to think about this when I read in Genesis 1:1 it said, God created and then in John 1 it tells us that the Word was with God and that the Word became flesh. The way I understand these scriptures I've just read is that it says that Jesus and God are one and the same."

Michael couldn't help himself he had to say something. "So you're saying Jesus and God are the same person. Man, I think you've lost it. That's impossible. No way am I am my Daddy. He definitely isn't me."

Smiling Matt looked at him and said, "I know it sounds a bit far fetched but when you put the scriptures together it is so plain. Just listen, okay."

Seeing him nod his head he continued, "So let's go to Matthew 16:18-19. The reason I am going here is I need to build a foundation so you'll understand the plan of salvation. In this passage Jesus is talking to Peter and it says, '*And I say also unto thee, That thou art Peter, and upon this rock I will build my church; and the gates of hell shall not prevail against it. And I will give unto thee the keys of the kingdom of heaven: and whatsoever thou shalt bind on earth shall be bound in heaven; and whatsoever thou shalt loose on earth shall be loosed in heaven.*' The Apostle Peter is very important in the Word of God and in the plan of salvation."

Lesley looked at him and said, "We need to hurry this up."

Matt nodded his head and continued, "So let's go to Acts 2:38 where the Apostle Peter is talking. I want you to remember this is who Jesus chose so let's listen to what he says on the day of Pentecost, 'Then Peter said unto them, *Repent, and be baptized every one of you in the name of Jesus Christ for the remission of sins, and ye shall receive the gift of the Holy Ghost.*' But let's continue and look at Acts 19:2-6 where Paul is talking, '*He said unto them, Have ye received the Holy Ghost since ye believed? And they said unto him, We have not so much as heard whether there be any Holy Ghost. And he said unto them, Unto what then were ye baptized? And they said, Unto John's baptism. Then said Paul, John verily baptized with the baptism of repentance, saying unto the people , that they should believe on him which should come after him, that is, on Christ Jesus. When they heard this they were baptized in the name of the Lord Jesus. And when Paul had laid his hands upon them, the Holy Ghost came on them; and they spake with tongues, and prophesied.'"*

Looking around he could see the Spirit of God moving on this small group of people so he stood up and said, "Let's all stand, first we need to repent. I mean every one of us, whether we think we're saved or not. After we do that we ask God to forgive us of our sins then I want you to raise your hands and ask God to give you this wonderful gift I've told you about. You see it's a gift that's free. Jesus already paid the price. He gave His life so that we would have a chance at life. The Holy Ghost scares some people but it's not scary. It is God coming to live in you. You see our bodies are the temple of God. We have to empty out all the dirt and the stuff we have accumulated from life so that He can come in and live in us. When He takes up residence our whole lives change. There is no hocus pocus involved. It is simply the Spirit of God. When you pray and worship God by telling Him how much you love Him that you want Him in your life. He will come in. When He starts to come in you'll feel your tongue start to do some strange things. That's God. No-one will be touching you except to pray for you on the forehead. We don't have enough people here and that's not how the Holy Ghost works. You just simply believe He will fill you with His Spirit and He will. But when your tongue starts to act strange just go with it. Don't worry about what it sounds like. Its worship to God and so important. After that if you haven't been baptized in Jesus name that's next. So let's pray."

Watching outside the Sherriff thought these people have got to be crazy. To think if my wife and son are alive they are probably in there. Raising his gun, he sighted in his wife and thought I could take her right now. As he pulled back on the trigger and the bullet released. He thought to himself, that will teach her to disobey me. As he watched the bullet go sailing toward the house he kept waiting for the sound of shattering glass but he never heard any. What he saw frightened him more than anything else. It was like a hand reached down and caught the bullet.

Shaking his head, he thought, no. I'm seeing things. No-one can catch a bullet. Continuing to look toward the house he raised his binoculars and sure enough they were standing with their hands raised like they were surrendering. But wait a minute, their eyes were closed and one man was walking around putting his hand on their foreheads. What is going on here? Are these people loony? Don't they know we're out here going to kill them all?

Where did that bullet go? There is no way something or someone caught it. Glancing over he knew he couldn't let anyone know what he saw or what he thought he saw. They'd haul him away and he'd spend the rest of his days in a mental ward.

The young angel looked at the older angel and said, "I thought we were supposed to wait and do nothing. I thought we had orders."

The older angel sighed and said, "Yes, we do have orders. I'm obeying those orders. I'm to stop anything from happening until they have all prayed. After that when the battle begins we will fight for them. They will know that their God saved their lives this day."

The young angel replied, "So what are our orders. Care to share with me."

"When the time comes I will but for now we wait."

In the living room suddenly a glory cloud filled the room as one by one they all repented and God filled them with the wonderful gift of the Holy Ghost of which the initial evidence of it is speaking in other tongues. As they lifted their voices to edify the King of Kings and the Lord of Lords heaven was rejoicing.

When Lesley began talking in that heavenly language she was sure she could feel her parents wrapping their arms around her once more urging her to get all she could get. So she prayed ever the more. When everyone finished Matt said, "Let's head upstairs where we've filled up the Jacuzzi to baptize all of you."

As they went into the water first it was Lesley who was so excited to get her sins washed away into the sea of forgetfulness where they would never be remembered against her, after her it was Ella, Michaels mother, and then Michael. As they came up out of the water worshipping God and giving Him glory they each knew that now the real test would come.

Knowing that they had little or no guns or ammunition they had no idea how they were to fight this battle. Lesley knew help was on the way but would arrive woefully late she said, "My parents told me when I was waking up this morning that the battle is not ours, but it is the Lords. We just have to trust him."

Matt said, "It's been a long morning and now we need to get in the car and go to church. I am here, after all, to try out to pastor this country church. I also feel like the battle is God's and that He will protect us as we go about our daily business. So let's hit the road for church."

Trusting God

As they loaded up it was decided they would all go in the Hummer. They wanted the people to know that were watching them that they were not afraid. They were stepping out in faith that God would walk before them and protect them as they traveled to church.

While Michael felt amazing light he also felt that they were being stupid by going out like this. He had heard everything they had said about God protecting them but he also felt like the good Lord expected you to use common sense and not be stupid by putting yourself in more danger. Also because he still had no clothes he was going to church in a hospital gown.

Ella, was looking around. In her heart she knew her husband was out in the woods and she knew this would be a slap in the face to him from her. She knew he would make her pay. She was ready now. She hadn't been ready before but now she knew where she would spend eternity so she could take whatever punishment he wanted to give her.

Darlene fingered her 45 as she walked to the Hummer. If shooting started she wanted to be able to shoot back and she was prepared. Looking in the trees she knew her husband was in one of them with an automatic rifle ready to start shooting. She knew they were woefully under manned but they had God on their side.

Lesley was right behind Darlene and had a gun in each hand. One hand held an automatic rifle and the other a 45. She also knew that if the firefight started right now they were sitting ducks. She did not like this feeling. It hadn't felt good on foreign soil and it felt even less so at home. Looking up she caught Matt's gaze and knew she loved him but would she ever have a chance to find out if he loved her?

Matt watched them come out as he sat in the driver's seat. He was ready to go once everyone was loaded. What they didn't know is he had stashed two automatic pistols in the visor and had one in his lap. He was armed to the teeth. His most important armor was lying on the armrest beside him. It was his Bible. The Word of God was his greatest comfort and biggest challenger. It challenged him daily to be better to do more no matter how he felt.

Thinking about the message God had given him for this morning he wondered how they would all take it. God had kept him up most of the night talking to him in prayer and inspiration. While he didn't' usually use notes when he ministered he had plenty of notes. He really doubted he would use them today but God had laid the groundwork for what he need to say that would help all of them, especially himself.

Once they were all in the SUV they prayed asking God for traveling mercies even though they were only going a few minutes down the road. They knew they needed God's protection because while the SUV had been checked over anything could have been put across the road, thrown at them or shot at them on the way. They knew what kind of chances they were taking by leaving the house but for some reason this was what God wanted them to do.

Matt couldn't believe it when God had let him know that he needed to convince everyone to go to church this morning. What was he thinking? Sighing to himself, he knew what he was thinking. He was thinking I have to obey God. It may not make sense to anyone else but I have to do this.

As they drove down the road the peaceful scenery that greeted them with the fruit trees swaying in the breeze and the livestock grazing on the hillsides hid any problems from the local community.

Arriving at the church they quickly slipped in. Matt looked at Lesley and said, "I know this is hard for you. I'm praying for you."

Lesley looked up at him and said, "Thank you for thinking about that."

She knew that very few men would realize how hard it might be for her to come to this church after all these years. She was so blessed God had placed Matt in her life if only for a few days to help her through this crisis and be able to move on to a more fulfilling life.

As church started and they sang the old songs out of the red hymnal that most churches can't find today. She loved hearing them sing, "When the roll is called up yonder I'll be there," and "It is Well With My Soul," lastly "I Need Thee". She thought to herself, there truly is no place like home. It was a church where when they sing from the hymnals they worship God. It was all coming back to her and quickly.

Then it was time for Matt to minister. This is when she realized they could never be together. Their lives were two different. She was a lawyer fighting crime in a big city, writing best sellers and he felt called to be a missionary. That was about as far from each other as you could get realistically.

Then Matt began by saying, "Let's turn to Matthew 6:14-15, 'For if ye forgive men their trespasses, your heavenly Father will also forgive you: But if ye forgive not men their trespasses, neither will your Father forgive your trespasses.' Now turn to Luke 23:34 where we will see what ultimate forgiveness looks like, 'Then Jesus said, Father forgive them; for they know not what they do. And they parted his raiment, and cast lots.'"

Pausing he looked around at the congregation and settled his gaze on Lesley because he knew this message was as hard for him to deliver as it would be for her to hear. Stepping back from the pulpit he said, "I have one other scripture to read and then I'll give you my title. Lastly let's look at Matthew 5:23-24, 'Therefore if thou bring thy gift to the altar, and there rememberest that thy brother hath ought against thee; Leave there thy gift before the altar, and go thy way; first be reconciled to thy brother and then come and offer thy gift."

Bowing his head he continued, "Let's pray. Lord today we know that this church and this group of people have been through a series of events that still haunt them today. We need to understand what true forgiveness is and how to exhibit it to those in need of it. While we all are facing challenges, tests and trials that we don't think anyone else can understand we know that whatever is going on in our lives you are in control and are taking care of us. We thank you Lord. Now, we ask you to touch us, to change us, to mold us and make us in your image. Let our hearts be anointed to hear what you have to say to us, precious Lord. We thank you for your inspiration and your power today. In Jesus name amen."

Knowing how hard this was for him when God started talking to him about it he knew it was going to be doubly hard for most of this congregation. While Lesley hadn't been welcomed with open arms this morning she hadn't been asked to leave by those who thought she was the devil. That was progress. Sometimes people in the church treat their own worse than others would treat their worst enemy just because they're different.

Smiling, he said, "Don't worry folks I'm not going to keep you long but God has given me a message for you. Jesus taught us by example how to forgive but we don't do what He taught. We tend to want to put our own spin on His words. If you will just read the words in red in your Bible you will find it very easy to follow and very straight forward. You don't need a preacher to tell you word for word what Jesus said. You're all smart people and can read. However, because you want to interpret what He said and not take it literally, well, that's why you need a preacher. Preachers become your conscience when you won't listen to your conscience. Think about that."

Seeing Lesley nod he continued, "Our conscience will preach to us when no-one else will, yet we manage to turn it off. We pick up the phone or we turn on the television, or the radio, or get on the internet. We'll do anything not to listen to our conscience or read our Bible."

Grinning he said, "You didn't know I was going there. You see even if you've been in church for fifty years when was the last time you and God really had an old fashioned prayer meeting where you met Him and talked with Him. He longs to hear your voice. I know you come to church two to three times a week. You teach Sunday School, sing in the choir, help out when it's needed but tell me when do you talk to your God? Does He know your voice? Would He recognize your voice? Or are you a stranger to Him? Is the only time you pray when you are in church? Do you have a time and a place where you pray every day by yourself? You see, when you get there then this forgiveness thing will be easy for you to do."

"We want to be forgiven but we've forgotten in order to be forgiven we must forgive. That's what my Bible says. What does your Bible say? Do you just want to be the judge? If you do I wouldn't want to be you. No matter what has happened to us in life or in church we must forgive. People in church tend to hurt each other worse than anyone else. We literally shoot our own wounded. We don't help them up, we kick them when they make mistakes. Forgiveness, true forgiveness will reach down and give them a hand up. Yes, they may hurt you again and if they do, you need to reach out again just like Jesus. You see, He is our example."

Walking from behind the pulpit he said, "I need to be the first one in the altar today because I need to let God know I forgive the people that have caused Lesley so much pain by taking her parents from her at the age of nine. I am angry that a little girl was robbed of her parents because someone wanted to make money and they got in the way because lives were being changed and transformed. I'm sure everyone here today has someone they need to forgive. You see that same Bible that tells us about Jesus forgiving them when He was hanging on the cross also tells us that if we know our brother has ought against us we are to take our gift to the altar and leave it there. We are then to go to our brother and ask for forgiveness. It doesn't matter if we did anything wrong. It's not about that. It's about forgiveness and being forgiven. The altar is open."

Walking to the altar and kneeling himself he had no idea if anyone else came but he knew he needed to clean himself up before God. When he got up he saw the altar was full. People were weeping and when he saw Lesley he saw her aunt and uncle with their arms wrapped around her. While he knew that all wouldn't be completely well with them for a while they were making a step in the right direction.

As church ended and he was meeting people he found everyone had enjoyed his simple but effective message that God had given him to give to them. Loading up he decided looking at his ragtag team that while he would have liked to have gone out to eat unfortunately one of them was in a hospital gown so back to the house they went. The closer they got to the house the quieter everyone in the car became because they did not know what they would be facing. They might not even be able to get back to the house.

Fortunately they had no problems getting back to the house but before they got out of the car his mom said, "Everyone, realize the house has probably been bugged again and maybe even booby trapped. We must be very careful where we step and what we do. These people are very evil. They are expert criminals. They intend for us not to make it out alive but all we have to remember is that God is on our side and those angels are with us with their flaming swords to protect us."

Lesley spoke up and said, "Let's eat and get ready for the siege. I would think tonight after midnight they'll rush in expecting to catch us off guard so we must be ready. If you see anything you think we could use as a weapon grab it and let's figure out what to do. In the meantime let's eat. I would think the power to the house would be cut off tonight."

Meanwhile flights were arriving in Morgantown and the team of special forces were getting together and making their plan of attack. They had no way of knowing what was going on or how soon it would all unfold but they had to wait on their entire team to get there before leaving.

The head of the team tried to contact Lesley but had no response. This worried him. It let him know that while the situation had been dangerous it was now dire. They needed to hurry if they wanted to be able to get them out alive.

Realizing he needed an army helicopter he put a call into another buddy. They found a helicopter. As soon as their last team mate arrived they would leave via helicopter for the final assent into battle. He had a feeling this was going to end badly. He wanted to be home by tomorrow morning kissing his newborn son.

That evening Lesley couldn't understand why her phone wasn't working. Looking at Matt she said, "We have no communication with the outside world." About then the lights blinked and went off. It's about to begin she thought to herself.

Grabbing the few weapons they had they took their places to watch the battle start. Matt looked at Lesley and said, "Can I talk to you for a minute?"

Lesley grinned and said, "Matt, I really don't think now is a good time to talk."

Winking at her he said, "Lesley, I know this is fast but I think I'm falling in love with you. I couldn't tell you until now. I just want you to know you're loved."

As tears puddled in her eyes she looked at him and replied, "Matt, you are so sweet. I've been fighting this pull towards you since that day on the plane. I don't know what is going on but if this is what falling in love feels like, I think I'm falling to."

Pulling her to him, he hugged her and gave her a kiss then said, "Let's pray. Lord we thank you for our friends that prayed today and received the gift of the Holy Ghost. We praise you and worship you for all you've done for us. You had Lesley tell us that the battle is not ours, but yours. Lord we could really use some reinforcements about now. We thank you and praise you for it in Jesus name."

Raising their heads they each wondered if when morning came who all would still be there and all in one piece to tell about this battle. Lesley knew in her heart that should she die tonight her parents were rejoicing in heaven because she had finally truly come home and laid her burdens at the feet of Jesus.

The Battle with Angelic Hosts

As the special force team ran and jumped into their helicopter they were all loaded down with weapons and explosive devices. They meant to conquer the enemy this night. It was so dark out in the rural countryside that you could cut it with a knife.

The leader of the group spoke into his mouthpiece which everyone had a headset on so they could hear him. He outlined his plan once they arrived on the scene. He also let them know they no longer had contact with Lesley so were unsure if the battle had already taken place. He wanted them to know they could be going in to retrieve bodies instead of releasing live hostages.

As they put their heads down he said, "I don't know why I'm doing this and I could get into trouble but since when has that stopped me?" As he heard them laughing, he continued, "Actually I do know why I'm doing this. I'm doing it because I remember Lesley doing it. It's her we're going into rescue so I want us to pray. Something bigger than us is going on right now and I believe if we pray God will change the outcome. That's what she always used to tell me so I'm going to believe that it's possible."

Not knowing how to pray he began, "God I know we haven't exactly been on speaking terms but Lesley is so much more than a comrade in arms. She is like a sister to most of us. We know whatever is going on in this town is evil but we also know her parent's loved you. So we're asking you on their behalf to keep her and whoever is with her safe until we can get there. Amen."

Opening his eyes he looked at them and said, "I don't know if that did any good but at least we did it. Now let's catch twenty winks before we get there."

Wondering how this would all work out Lesley was almost hit by a grenade as it came flying by her. Knowing they wouldn't know what it was she ran to it and grabbed it and hurled it back outside. About then what she saw standing outside amazed her. There were angels everywhere with flaming swords. Blinking her eyes she yelled to Matt, "Can you see this?"

"See what?"

"Look outside, all around us...."

Looking outside at first he could see nothing except the darkness then as his eyes adjusted he saw something funny. "What is it?"

"You're the preacher and you don't know? Where is your faith?"

Looking at Lesley he said, "I see some shadows but that's about it."

"LOOK AGAIN!!!"

Turning back to look outside again, he prayed in his mind, "God let me see what she sees."

Looking around he couldn't believe his eyes. The outside looked lit up like a city street during Christmas with angels holding flaming swords. No-one would believe this in their wildest imaginations. This stuff only happened in the Bible, not today. But I'm seeing it, he thought to himself. Then he looked at Lesley and realized she knew he'd just seen what she was seeing.

Grabbing her hand he said, "Let's sit down and watch the show.´ I think we're about ready to see heavenly fireworks. This battle truly belongs to God."

As the Sherriff and his team moved in under the cloak of darkness closer to the house they wondered where the lights were coming from. The power had been cut. He knew for sure because he had been the one to do it.

And where would they get that kind of glow. This was strange. As he continued heading toward the house he had a feeling this was going to be bad. But we'll win he thought to himself. We have to!

As the devil watched the battle unfold below he knew those wimpy angels could never win against the powers of darkness and his demons. He had been winning battles against people of faith for years. They are spineless most of the time and don't believe in the promises God gives them. Laughing to himself he thought I've bullied them for years and they've taken it. Tonight will be no different!

Why Lesley had to go against him after all these years and come back here was beyond anything he could figure out. He had been giving her nightmares since that fateful night and torturing her. Why, I've had so much fun making her miserable and she let me. I didn't even have to work hard at it.

As the Sherriff stood outside he thought, tonight would be the icing on the cake. Rubbing his hands together gleefully he couldn't wait to see her face when she was tortured and died. He wanted it to be slow and painful just like her parent's. He remembered them begging for their lives. It didn't do them any good. The decision had already been made. They had caused him too much trouble.

He had lost way too many to religion because of them. How some people could walk away from all the money they were making to live on faith. Yea, right, faith didn't pay the bills or put food on the table. Selling drugs did. He had even tried blackmailing the people who had gotten in church with their crimes. They went and confessed. They were stupid. They couldn't be smart. Well, tonight it would be over. This should have been finished thirty years ago, yet, here we are cleaning up another fine mess.

"Do you see what's going on now," the older angel asked the younger angel.

"Yes, I see evil is prepared to win this battle."

"What do you know will happen?"

"God will prevail."

"Yes, you are so right," the older angel replied, "God will prevail. We are the help they need right now. Are you ready?"

"Yes."

"Then let's go show them this battle truly belongs to God."

As the mafia and the others snuck closer to the house it was like they got to a point and could go no further. They couldn't understand it. Then when they looked up they saw these white beings with swords of fire.

As the swords came down on them they felt pain like no other as they passed out. They tried to shoot, throw grenades but it was all rendered useless. This took only a matter of minutes. When they came to they saw the white beings standing still with their swords. They wanted to run but they couldn't. They couldn't move.

About then they heard a helicopter landing. They thought help is here. They'll take these things out of here and get us up. At that point the house was surrounded by men dressed all in black. When they realized they didn't need to fight but arrest the people on the ground. They did just that.

As Lesley and her group watched from the house they could hardly believe their eyes. Instead of them having to fight a battle God had literally sent angels to fight their battle. When her team landed all they had to do was clean up. Looking outside she saw an angel turn, give her a wink and a wave as they disappeared.

Really, could an angel do that? Well, why not. If they could fight her battle for her I reckon they could wink.

Hearing her team rush the house she said, "Everyone raise your hands so they'll know we're the good guys."

Seeing her friend, John come towards her she threw herself into his arms and said, "Thank God you got here when you did."

"Well, it looks like we were too late for the fun."

"How did you get them to lay there on the ground until we got here?"

"Well, you see," looking at Matt and seeing him shake his head no, she thought to herself, it is so unbelievable that it's a believable story, "You're never going to believe this but we prayed…."

Interrupting her John said, "You prayed. You won't believe this but in the helicopter on the way here I prayed for you and for the team…"

Looking up she said, "Well, then, maybe you'll believe this."

She then told him the story of how they had sat and watched the battle outside fought by angels. She truly believed without God's help they would be dead now but God had stepped in and fought the battle.

Epilogue

Six years later Lesley leaned back in the seat and put her hand on Matt's. Rubbing his hand she looked up into those ocean blue eyes and said, "Can you believe it's been five years since we met on a plane just like this one coming in to the airport in Morgantown?"

"No, it's hard to believe. What's harder to believe is that we fell in love within days of meeting each other although we did wait a whole year to get married."

"Remember our wedding at my folks house. No-one could believe I wanted to get married there with everything that had happened but I feel so close to them there. I'm so glad I decided not to sell it and it's now a sanctuary for us and our children."

"Yes, and it's so nice to know that Ella is living there taking care of it for us while we are gone."

"And who would have ever dreamed Matt would become the pastor of that little country church. God sure does have a way of working things out as only He can do. "

"On, and, Matt, your mother, starting a ministry at her age? Please don't tell her I said that at her age... You know how she gets. She's a little touchy about her age."

Laughing, Matt responded, "Oh, yes, we never know where my folks are. Between us on the mission field, your books, my mother's ministry and the books she writes it's a wonder any of us get any sleep these days."

Then they looked between them at their three year old daughter, Anna Elizabeth and at the babies lying in their laps, the twin boys, Joshua and Caleb they both smiled.

Matt through eyes that glistened with tears of joy said, "Les, it's hard to believe we've been on the mission field for four years and have been married for five with three children and another one on the way. Who would have dreamed all this."

"I know," she said, " and that my team would all want to get to find out about Jesus. Grant it we still have a few hold outs but God's working on them. I still find it hard to believe how hard it is to sometimes trust God but when you do He just meets us where we are. Then He simply provides our needs. He sometimes even provides before we ask or before we know what to ask for. Just like when he put you beside me on that plane six years ago. God knew what He was doing. You've been my protector ever since."

"Ah, Les, it isn't like I had no idea how God was going to work it out but I knew He had to do it. You may not like this but I had promised God that I wouldn't ever marry anyone who didn't love God like I did or have a close walk with Him because of my ministry. I was so afraid I was going to have to walk away from you and I would have but then you found God again. I just love you and know how blessed I am everything worked out like it did. I remember looking into those dreamy green eyes with those red eyelashes and beautiful pale skin with those long legs of yours I was gone. I really had to pray."

"Matt, I knew you were that way. It doesn't bother me. I pray each and every one of our children get it like that so that no matter who comes into their life that they fall in love with they will love God more. That way it won't be a choice. The decision will be made before that happens. Let's pray right now for our children and their futures whatever God has for them."

As Matt and Lesley linked their hands and touched each of their three children and the one yet to be born on the same flight but six years later. They prayed for their little family that God would order their footsteps each and every day with obedience to Him and the Word of God like has not been seen often.

AVAILABLE

Sister Susan D. Smith

To come to your church

Or

Civic Organization

To inspire, to encourage and to share what God has done and continues to do

(304) 640-5717

Facebook: Susan D Wine Smith

Made in the USA
Columbia, SC
25 May 2018